THE SUPER MOM'S GUIDE TO

Simply Super Sweets and Treats for Every Season

Skyhorse Publishing books may be purchased in bulk at special discounts for sales promotion, corporate gifts, fund-raising, or educational purposes. Special editions can also be created to specifications. For details, contact the Special Sales Department, Skyhorse Publishing, 307 West 36th Street, 11th Floor, New York, NY 10018 or info@skyhorsepublishing.com.

Skyhorse® and Skyhorse Publishing® are registered trademarks of Skyhorse Publishing, Inc.®, a Delaware corporation.

Visit our website at www.skyhorsepublishing.com.

10 9 8 7 6 5 4 3 2 1

Library of Congress Cataloging-in-Publication Data is available on file.

Cover design by Danielle Ceccolini
Cover photo credit Nick Biliotti.

Print ISBN: 978-1-62914-568-6
Ebook ISBN: 978-1-63220-141-6

Printed in China

THE SUPER MOM'S GUIDE TO

Simply Super Sweets and Treats for Every Season

80 Cakes, Cookies, Pies, and Snacks for Perfectly Imperfect Moms

BY **DEBORAH STALLINGS STUMM**

Skyhorse Publishing

For Morgan and Dylan

My amazing kiddos who inspire me to be the best "Super Mom" I can be.

CONTENTS

Before We Get Started

Wow, It's Winter . . . Now What to Make?

Christmas, Hanukkah & the Holly Jolly Winter Holidays

My New Love, Valentine's Day

Celebrate Springtime

Critter Country

A Playful St. Patty's Day

Egg-ceptional Easter Treats

Mom Rocks and Dads & Grads Are on a Roll

Summer Fun
Simply, Super Summer

Hooray for the USA!

The Frenzy of Fall
Easy-Breezy Autumn

Spooktacular Halloween Sweets

New Traditions for Your Thanksgiving Table

Anytime Celebrations

ACKNOWLEDGMENTS

I am a firm believer in taking the path less traveled: sticking to your beliefs, persevering, and creating your own destiny. I have also come to realize that life can take you in directions you never imagined if you are ready to seize unexpected opportunities that are put in your path. This book is one of those opportunities.

The journey began twelve years ago when I resigned from my high profile job to get married, start a family, and try my hand at becoming an entrepreneur. The president of my company, in his typical arrogant form, said to me, "You're resigning?! What are you going to do? Get married, pop out some babies, and become Betty Crocker?" Had I not been stunned into silence, I would have said, "I can only hope to be fortunate enough to become a wife, a mother, and thought of as highly as one of the most well-respected brands in the country!" Life does have a funny way of working things out though, as I find myself blessed with a beautiful family and now a sweets and treats cookbook.

I would like to express my heartfelt appreciation to my husband, Mark, who has encouraged me to pursue my entrepreneurial spirit through thick and thin and has stood by me through the victories, tears, and anxiety that come with running your own business. My children, Morgan and Dylan, are my biggest cheerleaders and truly believe that their mom is a Super Mom. Please don't burst their bubble! My parents and sister are always wondering what crazy idea I am going to come up with next and have been wonderful sounding boards and support for me. To my best friend, Dani, who deserves a cookbook more than I do, I love you for your faith in me even though you are a much better cook than I am.

Courtney, you were with me as we developed the SuperMoms360.com concept and I can't imagine having started the journey without you. Ashton, thanks for being the yin to my yang, keeping me in balance and for bringing your best every day. Nick at Enne Bi Communications, thank you for taking such gorgeous pictures of our sweets and treats and making them the stars of the show. To my talented team past and present at Super Moms 360, Cleopatra, Stefanie, Amber, Monique, Rachael, David, Blaise, and Alex, your hard work is not forgotten. To my agent, Andrea, at Harvey Klinger, I connected with you from our first communication and felt that we were somehow kindred spirits. I appreciate your belief in me, your perseverance, and continued guidance. And to the team at Skyhorse Publishing, I am eternally grateful for the opportunity to share my voice and think that you all are simply . . . . . . super!

Introduction
Confessions of an Imperfect Mom

I'll admit it—I am intimidated by the moms who can do it all. You know the ones—the ones who have an immaculate home; the ones who look like a "ten" when they drop their kids off at school; the ones that make amazing customized cupcakes (from scratch of course!) for their kids' birthday parties. Maybe I am just missing the "cooking gene," but I have never been very comfortable in the kitchen. In fact, if there was an award in high school for the "Least Likely to Write a Cookbook," I would have been a shoo-in for the honor. Even back then, I burned the brownies I baked for my boyfriend and had trouble making a grilled cheese. Flash forward a few years (or twenty …) and even after watching all the chef shows and buying the fancy cookbooks, I still don't know how to candy a kumquat or create a masterpiece with fondant.

When my kids started school, I quickly realized that expectations were high and time was short when it came to children's parties and family celebrations. I would dash to the store to buy cupcakes for the classroom party, display them on my own plate, and cross my fingers that nobody noticed. After comparing myself one too many times to the moms who spent hours in the kitchen and feeling like I was letting my kids down, I came up with a simple solution: I started to explore making easy but adorable treats that were partially homemade. Most of them didn't even involve baking and took no time at all. This kernel of an idea led to the development of my website, SuperMoms360.com, *The Busy Mom's Guide to Being Simply . . . Super!* I quickly realized that my ideas were resonating with other busy moms and it fueled my desire to share my discoveries.

Simply Super Sweets and Treats for Every Season is a compilation of my recipes, tips, and tricks so overscheduled moms everywhere can look like stars without breaking a sweat!

If you are a mom who is truly amazing, these recipes may be a little too simple for your taste. But for the rest of us who are *perfectly imperfect*, I hope you will find these little sweets and treats to be fun, festive, and stress-free. Please enjoy *Simply Super Sweets and Treats for Every Season!*

BEFORE WE GET STARTED

As a mom and a business woman I am used to making rules and creating guidelines. Here are a few that I would like to establish up front before you dive into this book.

1. I am an imperfect mom.

2. My ideas are not intended to replace decadent recipes made from scratch or family traditions that have been passed down for generations. These are simple solutions that are meant to help out busy moms who are short on time.

3. You will notice that some of the recipes use approximate quantities and offer multiple choices for ingredients. I am a firm believer in using what you can find in your pantry and embracing flexibility.

4. No, these recipes are not completely foolproof. I will admit that I had to try some of them a few times before they turned out the way I wanted. I've included tips along with the recipes to help you learn from some of my mistakes.

5. Yes, you are probably a better cook than I am.

6. I am a firm believer in promoting healthy eating for kids. The seasonal recipes included in this book are intended to be eaten in moderation and for special occasions. I am "that mom" who allows my kids only one piece of Halloween candy per day and insists on fruit and vegetables with every meal.

7. I hope you find these recipes to be helpful—without all the hassle. They use easy-to-find ingredients and items you already have at home. Combine them with a little love and you'll be done in a snap! You GO Super Mom!

Staples for Simply
Super Sweets

There is something to be said about having "go-to" items in your pantry that can be turned into multiple materpieces in a snap. How many times have we heard, "Mom, I need to bring treats for the party . . . and it's *tomorrow*!!" Really? Are you kidding me right now?!

I don't recommend becoming a hoarder and keeping every ingredient on hand (okay, truth be told I *am* a pantry pack-rat . . . just ask my husband!), but I do have some favorite items that have helped me in a pinch on many occasions.

- Hershey's Kisses
- A large bag of plain M&M'S Chocolate Candies— you can pick out the colors you need
- Nutter Butter cookies—who knew how many things you could make with these?
- OREO or chocolate sandwich cookies
- Chocolate-covered shortbread cookies
- Pretzel rods
- Milk chocolate chips
- White chocolate baking chips or candy melts

- Large marshmallows
- Container of chocolate frosting
- Seasonal colored sprinkles
- Candy eyes—give your critters personality
- Decorator icing/gel in multiple colors
- A can of green cupcake icing with decorator tips included—Betty Crocker and Wilton both make versions that I like
- Bamboo skewers
- Seasonal cookie cutters (hearts, stars, holiday shapes)

Even if you don't have these items on hand, you'll find that the treats in this book use ingredients that can easily be found in your local grocery store. Far be it from me to add extra "to-dos" to your already maxed out list!

Wow, It's Winter . . .

NOW WHAT TO MAKE?

There's just something about winter that draws out my hibernating creativity. It may be that it's so cold outside that we are looking for activities to warm our souls. The world is filled with twinkling lights, holiday music, young children's anticipation, and, of course, extra stress. With a calendar full of Christmas celebrations, Hanukkah gatherings, classroom parties, and never enough hours to check everything off our lists, it's the perfect time of year for some simply super sweets and treats. Since the kids are out of school for a few weeks, these recipes can double as crafts and be a surefire way to keep them busy while spending quality time together as a family. The recipes included in this chapter cover some of my favorite winter holidays: Christmas, Hanukkah, and Valentine's Day. I've included tips for each one to help you avoid mistakes that I've made, adapt the recipes for your guests, and squeeze in some quality time with your kids while you're at it. Pretty super, right?

CHRISTMAS, HANUKKAH & THE HOLLY JOLLY WINTER HOLIDAYS

If you are like me, the holidays bring out my holly and sometimes not-so-jolly side. In theory, we should be enjoying every minute of the season. In reality, it's one of the most stressful times of the year for moms with the present-buying, guest-hosting, and cooking. The treats in this section are super easy and use only a few ingredients. Not that it's a competition (okay, it's a *little* bit of a competition), but try bringing some of these to an upcoming family-friendly Christmas party, Hanukkah gathering, or holiday celebration and let's *see* whose treats get eaten first! Wink.

CHRISTMAS CEREAL WREATHS

Makes 18–24

These crunchy and chewy holiday treats will sweeten even the most decadent cookie trays. No need to tell your host that you made them in less than 15 minutes!

What You'll Need

- ¼ CUP MARGARINE OR BUTTER
- 1 BAG MINI OR REGULAR MARSHMALLOWS
- 7 CUPS CORN FLAKES
- GREEN FOOD COLORING
- RED CINNAMON DROP CANDIES
- WAX PAPER

Simple Instructions

Melt margarine in a microwave-safe bowl for 30 seconds. Add marshmallows and melt for approximately 1½ minutes, stirring every 30 seconds. Stir until smooth and completely melted. Add 8–10 drops of green food coloring to melted marshmallows and stir until blended. Add more food coloring if you like until the marshmallow mixture is the color you desire. Add corn flakes and stir until entirely coated.

Cover the cookie sheet with wax paper. Drop by rounded spoonfuls onto the wax paper. If they are very sticky, wait a few minutes and then make a hole in the center of each dollop by using the handle end of a spoon. Add 3–4 cinnamon drop candies to decorate. Let cool.

LEARN FROM MY MISTAKES: BEWARE OF THE BUTTER! I'M USUALLY A FAN OF IMPROVISING WITH INGREDIENT QUANTITIES BUT ADDING TOO MUCH BUTTER OR MARGARINE TO THESE WILL MAKE THEM TOO GOOEY TO SET UP CORRECTLY.

OH-SO-EASY
SANTA COOKIES

Makes 24 cookies

The Ho Ho holidays bring the promise of Santa and all his wonder. Fill your Christmas table with these Oh-So-Easy Santa Cookies that make a festive addition to any celebration.

Simple Instructions

Attach the star tip to the white decorator icing. Cover the top quarter of the cookie with a small amount of the white frosting, smooth with a knife, and cover with the red sugar sprinkles. Use the white frosting again to apply the white trim at the bottom of Santa's hat and the ball at the top. Use a small dab of the icing to secure two mini chocolate chips for Santa's eyes and one cinnamon drop candy for his nose. Create Santa's beard by using multiple quick pulses of the white frosting as this will give the beard a textured look. Display on a red or Christmas-themed serving platter.

What You'll Need

- 24 NUTTER BUTTER COOKIES
- 1 CAN WHITE CUPCAKE ICING WITH DECORATOR TIPS INCLUDED
- 48 MINI CHOCOLATE CHIPS
- 24 RED CINNAMON DROP CANDIES
- RED SUGAR SPRINKLES

LEARN FROM MY MISTAKES: WHEN CREATING THESE SUPER-CUTE SANTAS, START FROM THE TOP AND WORK YOUR WAY TO THE BOTTOM. YOU DON'T WANT SANTA'S BEARD TO END UP ALL OVER THE BACK OF YOUR HAND.

Reindeer
Pops

Makes 24 pops

You can't have Christmas without Santa's reindeer! These silly and super easy chocolate-covered Reindeer Pops will add personality to all your holiday festivities.

Simple Instructions

Break the pretzels into the shape of antlers. This can take a little practice so make sure you have extra pretzels handy for the ones that don't work out quite right. Pour the milk chocolate chips into a microwave-safe bowl and melt for 1½–2 minutes on 70 percent power until smooth, stirring every 30 seconds. While the chocolate is melting, insert cookie pop sticks into the bottom of each marshmallow. When the chocolate has completely melted and is smooth, dip the marshmallow pops into the chocolate, completely coating the marshmallow and smoothing with a spoon.

Cover the baking sheet with wax paper. Place a pair of pretzel "antlers" in position on the wax paper and lay the chocolate-coated marshmallow on top to secure. Place two candy eyes and a cinnamon drop nose on each to make the face. Let the chocolate set by placing them in the refrigerator for an hour before removing from the wax paper.

What You'll Need

- 1 BAG LARGE PRETZEL TWISTS
- 1 BAG MILK CHOCOLATE CHIPS
- 24 LARGE MARSHMALLOWS
- 24 COOKIE POP STICKS
- 48 SUGAR CANDY EYES
- 24 CINNAMON DROP CANDIES
- WAX PAPER
- COOKIE PAN

SUPER MOM SAYS: TRY DISPLAYING THESE RED-NOSED REINDEER IN A FESTIVE HOLIDAY VASE TO MAKE CENTERPIECES THAT TURN INTO A DELICIOUS SNACK!

Christmas Tree
WAFFLES

Surprise your kids with these foolproof and festive waffles on Christmas morning or anytime during the holiday season. If you have a famous family waffle recipe, go ahead and use it. If not, boxed waffle mix works just fine.

What You'll Need

- WAFFLE MIX AND INGREDIENTS TO PREPARE (WATER, OIL, EGG, ETC.)
- GREEN FOOD COLORING
- FRUIT FOR DECORATIONS— BLUEBERRIES AND RASPBERRIES MAKE FABULOUS "ORNAMENTS"
- SPRINKLES (OPTIONAL)
- WHIPPED CREAM IN CAN
- NON-STICK COOKING SPRAY
- CIRCLE WAFFLE MAKER

Simple Instructions

Prepare waffle batter according to the directions on the box. Add 8–10 drops of green food coloring to the batter and stir. Continue to add food coloring until it is your desired color. Preheat the waffle iron and spray with non-stick cooking spray when ready. Pour approximately 1/3 cup of batter into the waffle maker and cook until ready. Remove from the waffle iron and separate into fourths. Layer 3–4 waffle triangles on a plate with the point at the top to look like a Christmas tree. Decorate with fresh berries, sprinkles, and whipped cream.

SUPER MOM SAYS: WHILE COOKING THE WAFFLES, BE CAREFUL NOT TO OVER-BROWN. AN EXTRA MINUTE OR TWO COULD CAUSE YOUR EVERGREEN TO LOOK EVER-BROWN LIKE THE DAY YOUR TREE GOES TO THE RECYCLING CENTER AFTER CHRISTMAS.

POWDERED SUGAR
Snowmen

Makes 12

These frosty fun Powdered Sugar Snowmen are the perfect addition to your child's classroom party, holiday sweets table, or just a cool treat the kids can enjoy throughout winter.

What You'll Need

- 36 MINI POWDERED SUGAR DONUTS
- 12 BAMBOO SKEWERS
- 12 PIECES CANDY CORN
- BLACK DECORATOR ICING
- 24 COLORED GUMDROPS
- 1 CAN COLORED CUPCAKE ICING (WITH DECORATOR TIPS INCLUDED)

Simple Instructions

Start by stacking three powdered donuts on a bamboo skewer. Insert the skewer carefully so the donuts don't crumble. Place a candy corn vertically into the hole in the top donut as the "carrot" nose. Draw two dots for the eyes and several dots for the smile with the black decorator icing. Place a gumdrop in each of the other two holes in the donuts as buttons. Using the can of cupcake icing with the flat tip, draw a horizontal line between the first and second donut for the scarf and then continue the line down one side for the scarf's tail. Display on a flat serving tray and garnish with ornaments and other fun holiday decorations.

ORNA-MINTS

Makes 24

Need to make some Christmas cookies in a snap? These simply super holiday treats can be done in minutes using only a few simple ingredients.

What You'll Need

- 24 CHOCOLATE-COVERED MINT COOKIES (WE USE KEEBLER GRASSHOPPER MINT CHOCOLATE COOKIES)
- 1 CONTAINER CHOCOLATE FROSTING
- HOLIDAY SPRINKLES
- COLORED DECORATOR GEL
- 24 MINI MARSHMALLOWS

Simple Instructions

Start by spreading a thin layer of chocolate frosting over the top of each cookie you would like to decorate with sprinkles. Embellish with sprinkles in a variety of patterns. You can also apply decorator gel in words or designs directly to the cookies if you prefer. Try doing some of each. After the decorating is done, apply a small amount of chocolate frosting to the top center of each cookie and attach a mini marshmallow. Store the cookies in a single layer, not overlapping, in an airtight container and then place into the refrigerator to set.

GET THE KIDS INVOLVED: THESE MINTY TREATS DOUBLE AS AN ART PROJECT FOR YOUR KIDS WHILE THEY ARE OUT ON WINTER BREAK. HAVE THEM USE THEIR IMAGINATIONS TO CREATE FUN HOLIDAY DESIGNS.

Peppermint Candy Cookies

Makes 12–18 cookies

Add a pop of color to your dessert table this Christmas with these Peppermint Candy Cookies that are a twist on the ever-popular peanut butter blossoms many of us have enjoyed since childhood.

What You'll Need

- 1 TUBE PRE-MADE REFRIGERATED SUGAR COOKIE DOUGH (YOU CAN ALSO MAKE YOUR OWN DOUGH, IF YOU PREFER)
- 1 CONTAINER RED SUGAR SPRINKLES
- 1 CONTAINER GREEN SUGAR SPRINKLES
- 1 PACKAGE PEPPERMINT HERSHEY'S KISSES

Simple Instructions

Preheat the oven according to the directions on the cookie dough package. Slice the pre-made sugar cookie dough into 12–18 slices and roll each one into a ball. Pour red sprinkles onto a plate and green sprinkles onto another plate. Roll half of the dough balls in the red sugar sprinkles and the other half in the green sugar sprinkles until they are completely coated.

Place the balls about 2 inches apart on an ungreased cookie sheet and bake according to the directions on the package. Unwrap the peppermint Hershey's Kisses while the cookies are baking. As soon as the cookies come out of the oven, gently press a peppermint Kiss into the center of each cookie while they are still hot. Let cool completely.

GET THE KIDS INVOLVED: AS LONG AS YOU DON'T MIND A LITTLE COLORED SUGAR ON YOUR FLOOR (OUR FAMILY DOGS HELP WITH THE CLEANUP!), THIS IS A PERFECT RECIPE TO GET YOUR LITTLE ELVES INVOLVED. HAVE THEM ROLL THE DOUGH IN THE SPRINKLES AND KEEP THEM BUSY COUNTING, SORTING, AND UNWRAPPING THE KISSES.

Rudolph Sugar
COOKIES

Makes 12–18 cookies

These simple-to-make cookies are sure to be a hit at your child's classroom holiday celebration and also can be an easy last-minute treat to bring to any family gathering.

What You'll Need

- 1 TUBE PRE-MADE REFRIGERATED SUGAR COOKIE DOUGH
- 36 CHOCOLATE-COVERED PRETZELS (WE USED FLIPZ MILK CHOCOLATE-COVERED PRETZELS)
- M&M'S CHOCOLATE CANDIES OR OTHER CANDY-COATED CHOCOLATE DROPS (RED FOR NOSE AND BLUE, GREEN, AND BROWN FOR EYES)

Simple Instructions

Cut the sugar cookie dough into 12–18 slices. Place on a cookie sheet and bake according to package instructions. Let the cookies cool for 1–2 minutes after removing from the oven. Place chocolate covered pretzels on the top left and right sides of the cookie for antlers. Then use two brown, blue, or green M&M'S for Rudolph's eyes and one red M&M for Rudolph's red nose. Let cool completely and store in an airtight container.

QUALITY TIME WITH THE KIDS: WHILE THE COOKIES ARE BAKING, HAVE YOUR LITTLE ONES SORT THE CANDIES INTO RED, GREEN, BLUE, AND BROWN PILES FOR YOU. IF THEY ARE OLD ENOUGH, THEY CAN ALSO HELP DECORATE THE COOKIES WHEN THEY COME OUT OF THE OVEN.

Hot Cocoa Candy Canes

Makes 12

ADD SOME FESTIVE FLAVOR TO YOUR HOT COCOA THIS HOLIDAY SEASON WITH MARSHMALLOW CANDY CANES. HOT COCOA CANDY CANES MAKE A GREAT DISPLAY FOR YOUR DESSERT TABLE OR HOT COCOA AND COFFEE STATION.

What You'll Need

- 12 LARGE MARSHMALLOWS
- 24 MINIATURE PEPPERMINT CANDY CANES
- 1 BAG MILK CHOCOLATE OR SEMI-SWEET CHOCOLATE CHIPS

LEARN FROM MY MISTAKES: CHOCOLATE WAS MY INITIAL NEMESIS FOR THIS RECIPE. IF YOUR MELTED CHOCOLATE IS A BIT TOO RUNNY AND THE CANDY CANE PIECES WON'T STICK OR SEEM TO DRIP, LET EACH CHOCOLATE MARSHMALLOW REST ON WAX PAPER FOR 1–2 MINUTES BEFORE TRYING TO COAT IT IN THE PEPPERMINT. YOU CAN ALSO PUT THE FINISHED HOT COCOA CANDY CANES INTO THE REFRIGERATOR FOR 10–15 MINUTES TO SET.

Simple Instructions

Prepare the marshmallows for dipping by placing the straight end of a miniature candy cane into the top of each marshmallow. This makes it very easy for dipping into the melted chocolate. Crush the additional candy canes in a plastic bag using a rolling pin or poultry mallet until they are in small pieces. Place the crushed candy canes into a bowl. Melt the chocolate chips in a microwave-safe bowl on 70–80 percent power for 1½–2 minutes, stirring every 30 seconds. Repeat until completely melted. Dip the marshmallow into the melted chocolate until the bottom and sides are completely coated, using a spoon to help cover and smooth. Roll each chocolate-covered marshmallow in the crushed candy canes. Serve with hot cocoa.

CHEERY CHEESE
Santas

Makes 12

These Christmas treats require only three ingredients and are packed with calcium. They are a great alternative to more traditional party sweets.

What You'll Need
- 12 MINI BABYBEL ORIGINAL CHEESE WHEELS
- BLACK EDIBLE MARKER
- 1 CONTAINER WHIPPED CREAM CHEESE

Simple Instructions

Open the Mini Babybel cheese wheels and leave the top half of the wax on the cheese. Draw eyes on the cheese with the food marker and roll a nose out of a small piece of red wax from the removed wrapper. Using a knife, dab cream cheese (whipped works best) on the bottom half of the cheese to make a beard and to the bottom of Santa's hat. Use a small dollop of cream cheese on the top center of the red wax to finish making the hat.

SUPER MOM SAYS: THESE TREATS ONLY HAVE THREE INGREDIENTS. CHEATING? MAYBE. BUT JUST THINK ABOUT HOW SMART (AND STRESS-FREE) YOU'LL FEEL WALKING INTO YOUR CHILD'S CLASSROOM WITH THESE LITTLE GUYS ON YOUR PLATTER!

Holly Jolly

JUICE

Serves 6–8

Need a festively easy drink to serve at your holiday celebration? Look no further as this beautiful beverage will brighten any party.

What You'll Need

- 1 (2 QT) BOTTLE CRANBERRY/RASPBERRY JUICE
- 1 (1 QT) BOTTLE PLAIN OR FLAVORED SPARKLING WATER
- 1 SMALL CONTAINER RASPBERRIES (FRESH OR FROZEN)
- 1 BOTTLE CHAMPAGNE (OPTIONAL)

Simple Instructions

Fill up a clear glass three-quarters full with chilled cranberry/raspberry juice and top with sparkling water. For adults, add champagne to taste. Top with 3 raspberries.

SUPER MOM SAYS:
IF YOU ARE HOSTING A HOLIDAY PARTY, HOLLY JOLLY JUICE MAKES A GREAT SIGNATURE COCKTAIL WHEN YOU SPIKE IT WITH A LITTLE CHAMPAGNE. JUST BE SURE TO KEEP THIS "MOMMY JUICE" IN A DIFFERENT SPOT THAN THE KIDS' REFRESHMENTS!

Delicious
Chocolate Dreidels

Makes 24

MAKE HANUKKAH EVEN
HAPPIER WITH THESE
UNBELIEVABLY EASY CHO-
COLATE DREIDELS THAT
CELEBRATE THE TREASURED
CHILDREN'S GAME.

What You'll Need
- 24 HERSHEY'S KISSES
  (UNWRAPPED)
- 24 MINI MARSHMALLOWS
- 1 BAG PRETZEL STICKS OR
  CHOW MEIN NOODLES
- 1 CONTAINER CHOCOLATE
  FROSTING
- BLUE AND WHITE SPRINKLES OR
  DECORATOR GEL/FROSTING

SUPER MOM SAYS:
SERIOUSLY, THIS MIGHT
BE ONE OF THE EASIEST
RECIPES YOU WILL FIND
FOR A HANUKKAH
CELEBRATION. OKAY,
MAYBE EVEN ANY
CELEBRATION.

Simple Instructions

Unwrap 24 of the Hershey's Kisses. Use a small amount of chocolate frosting as glue and place one mini marshmallow on the flat side of the chocolate Kiss. Break each pretzel stick or chow mein noodle into two pieces. Insert one piece into each marshmallow. If desired, use chocolate frosting to "glue" a sprinkle decoration onto the chocolate Kiss or add a design with decorator gel or frosting.

MY NEW LOVE, VALENTINE'S DAY

I'll be the first to admit that I've always thought Valentine's Day was overrated. I'm not one who demands hundred-dollar roses delivered to my door or a five-star meal at an overly-inflated price. Valentine's Day seems, well, a bit contrived. That was until I had children. There's something so endearing about your kids confiding in you about their first crush, drawing hearts on everything they can find, and bringing home special art projects that say "I love you, Mommy." For me, the holiday has taken on a new meaning and brought opportunities to explore creatively simple ideas that kids can enjoy all season long. In this section, you'll find easy classroom party treats that will brighten any table without dampening your mood while you make them. I've included traditional sweets (with a simply super flair, of course) along with some healthier alternatives, and even a few Valentine's Day brunch ideas. Get your heart-shaped cookie cutters ready!

SWEETHEART CINNAMON ROLLS

Makes 16 small or 8 large

Start your Valentine's Day morning with some lovin' from the oven. You won't believe how easy these are to make and they use only one ready-made ingredient.

What You'll Need
- 1 PACKAGE (TUBE) OF REFRIGERATED PRE-MADE CINNAMON ROLLS WITH FROSTING (USE REGULAR CINNAMON ROLLS INSTEAD OF THE MORE DELUXE VARIETIES)

LEARN FROM MY MISTAKES: THE FIRST TIME I MADE THESE, I DECIDED TO BE FANCY AND BOUGHT THE ULTRA-DELUXE, EXTRA CINNAMON-Y, EXTRA GOOEY, EXTRA EVERYTHING BRAND. THEY WERE DIFFICULT TO UNROLL AND I GAVE MYSELF A "B-" FOR THE END RESULT. THE NEXT TIME I BOUGHT THE GENERIC, BASIC CINNAMON ROLLS AND THEY TURNED OUT PERFECT! WELL AT LEAST A SOLID "A" FOR EFFORT.

Simple Instructions

Preheat oven to 325°F (or follow baking temperature on package). Open the tube and separate into individual rolls. Unroll each piece of dough and then cut it in half. If you prefer larger cinnamon rolls, you can use a whole piece instead of a half. One at a time, pinch the middle of the dough to form the bottom point of the heart. Then, roll the ends inward to form the shape of a heart. Mold to your liking. Bake on an ungreased cookie sheet for 10–11 minutes or according to package instructions. Remove from oven and let cool for about 5 minutes. Spread the frosting on each cinnamon roll and serve warm.

Berry Sweet
WAFFLES

Treat your kids to a love-you-a-bunch brunch with these super easy Valentine's Day waffles. Add some low-fat yogurt and fresh berries to complete this balanced breakfast.

What You'll Need
- STRAWBERRY FROZEN WAFFLES (OR WAFFLE FLAVOR OF YOUR CHOICE)
- LOW-FAT YOGURT— STRAWBERRY, RASPBERRY, OR OTHER BERRY FLAVOR
- FRESH STRAWBERRIES, RASPBERRIES, BLUEBERRIES, OR OTHER FRUIT
- LARGE HEART-SHAPED COOKIE CUTTER (NO LARGER THAN THE WAFFLE)

Simple Instructions
Toast the waffles in a toaster. Place each waffle on a flat surface and firmly press the cookie cutter into the waffle to create a heart shape. Trim off the excess on the sides. Top with low-fat yogurt and berries and serve.

Make as many as needed.

SUPER MOM SAYS: I'M PRETTY SURE THAT THIS DOESN'T EVEN COUNT AS COOKING. DOES IT REALLY MATTER, THOUGH? MY KIDS WENT BALLISTIC WHEN I MADE THESE FOR THE FIRST TIME AND SAID THAT I WAS "THE BEST COOK EVER!" I'M NOT PLANNING TO BURST THEIR BUBBLE ANY TIME SOON.

SWEET BROWNIE SANDWICHES

Makes 4-6

These sweet little sandwich brownies are a delightful addition to Valentine's Day. They are delicious to eat and even more fun to display on your party buffet.

What You'll Need
- 1 PACKAGE BROWNIE MIX AND INGREDIENTS TO PREPARE (I.E. WATER, OIL, EGG)
- HEART-SHAPED COOKIE CUTTER— MEDIUM SIZED
- 1 CONTAINER STRAWBERRY CAKE FROSTING (OR OTHER PINK, WHITE OR RED FLAVOR)
- VALENTINE'S DAY SPRINKLES
- FRESH RASPBERRIES TO GARNISH (OPTIONAL)
- 9 X 13-INCH BAKING PAN

SUPER MOM SAYS: I ALMOST FEEL LIKE A *REAL* BAKER WHEN I MAKE THESE BEAUTIFUL LITTLE BROWNIES. THEY ARE SO PRETTY WITH THEIR PINK FROSTING CENTERS, I ALMOST FORGET HOW EASY THEY ARE TO MAKE.

Simple Instructions

Preheat the oven using instructions on the brownie mix box. Prepare the brownie batter according to package instructions. Pour into a 9 x 13-inch pan and bake being careful not to over or under bake. Remove from oven and cool completely. Gently use the heart cookie cutter to make as many heart shapes as possible. Remove from pan. Generously spread the cake frosting on the inside of one of the brownie hearts. Top with the second heart. Add Valentine's Day sprinkles all the way around the frosting. Place all the completed heart-shaped brownie sandwiches on a serving tray and garnish with fresh raspberries if desired.

Cupid's Cookie
POPS

Makes 8-12

Bring out your inner artist with these absolutely adorable cookies on a stick. They make fun party favors or can be bundled together as a cookie bouquet and turned into a great gift idea.

What You'll Need

- 1 TUBE PRE-MADE REFRIGERATED SUGAR COOKIE DOUGH (YOU CAN ALSO MAKE YOUR OWN SUGAR COOKIE DOUGH)
- HEART-SHAPED COOKIE CUTTER, MEDIUM-SIZED
- 12 COOKIE POP STICKS OR POPSICLE STICKS
- CAKE OR COOKIE FROSTING—PINK, WHITE, OR RED
- SPRINKLES, SHREDDED COCONUT, DECORATING GEL, OR ANY EDIBLE DECORATIONS YOU LIKE

Simple Instructions

Preheat the oven per the cookie dough box instructions. Flour a clean, dry surface and roll out cookie dough to approximately ¼-inch thick. Press the heart-shaped cookie cutter into the dough and trim the edges. Place approximately 6 cookie pop sticks on each baking sheet leaving ample space in between. Transfer each dough heart using a spatula and gently place on top of a cookie stick with at least 1½–2 inches of dough overlapping the stick. Press down gently on the cookie dough to ensure the stick will attach while baking. Leave at least 1 inch between each cookie on the pan as they will expand when baking. If you are planning to decorate the cookies with sprinkles and no frosting, decorate the top of each cookie before baking. If you prefer to frost the cookies, bake according to package directions. Let cool on the baking sheet for 2 minutes, then gently use a spatula to remove from the pan and place on aluminum foil. Decorate with frosting and sprinkles as desired once completely cooled. Store the cookies in an air-tight container to keep fresh.

QUALITY TIME WITH THE KIDS: IF PATIENCE IS ONE OF YOUR VIRTUES, MAKING THESE COOKIE POPS WITH YOUR KIDS CAN BE AN OUTSTANDING OUTLET FOR YOUR BUDDING PICASSOS. JUST BE SURE THE BATH WATER IS WARM AND READY AFTERWARD TO WASH OFF THE EXTRA FROSTING.

Chocolate
Lovers Cookies

Makes 36 cookies

WHO KNEW THAT COOKIES MADE SO EASILY COULD COME OUT SO CUTE? THESE BITE-SIZED GOODIES ARE AN IDEAL ADDITION TO ANY VALENTINE'S DAY PARTY WHEN YOU ONLY HAVE MINUTES TO SPEND MAKING THEM.

What You'll Need

- 1 BAG MILK CHOCOLATE CHIPS OR CHOCOLATE CANDY MELTS
- 1 PACKAGE OREO COOKIES OR OTHER CHOCOLATE SANDWICH COOKIES
- 1 BAG WHITE CHOCOLATE CHIPS OR WHITE CANDY MELTS
- VALENTINE'S DAY SPRINKLES
- WAX PAPER

LEARN FROM MY MISTAKES: WASHING BOWLS AND CONTAINERS WITH HARDENED MELTED CHOCOLATE CAN BE A CHORE. AFTER LOSING MY PATIENCE AND THROWING AWAY MULTIPLE PLASTIC CONTAINERS, I FINALLY FIGURED OUT THE TRICK! USE HOT WATER AND CLEAN UP IS QUICK.

Simple Instructions

In a microwave-safe container, melt the milk chocolate chips at 80 percent power for 1½–2 minutes, stirring every 45 seconds. Meanwhile, divide the cookies into two groups. Once the chocolate is smooth, dip the first group in chocolate and smooth and shape with a spoon. Lay flat on wax paper and decorate with sprinkles. Next, melt the white chocolate chips or white candy melts in a different microwave-safe container at 60–70 percent power for 1½–2 minutes, stirring every 45 seconds. Repeat the process of dipping and smoothing the remaining cookies and then adding sprinkles. Cool in the refrigerator for at least 30 minutes to set.

Stained Glass
SWEETHEART COOKIES

Makes 18-24 cookies

Show your heart to your loved ones with these deliciously delightful cookies. The simulated stained glass will light up any Valentine's Day celebration.

What You'll Need

- 1 BAG SUGAR COOKIE MIX (AND INGREDIENTS TO PREPARE: EGG AND BUTTER OR MARGARINE)
- 24 JOLLY RANCHER CANDIES IN RED, PINK OR PURPLE
- ¼ CUP FLOUR
- 1 MEDIUM-LARGE HEART-SHAPED COOKIE CUTTER
- 1 SMALL HEART-SHAPED COOKIE CUTTER
- WAX PAPER
- ROLLING PIN

Simple Instructions

Preheat the oven according to the cookie mix instructions for cutout cookies. Select the color of Jolly Rancher candies that you would like to use (pink, red, purple, etc.). Put 8–10 Jolly Ranchers of the same color into a plastic bag and break them into smaller pieces by gently pounding them with a rolling pin or poultry mallet or another hard object. Prepare the cookie mix as directed on the package. Use flour to prevent sticking and roll out the dough until it's about ¼-inch thick. Use the larger heart cookie cutter first and then follow with the smaller heart in the middle. Remove the cutout from the smaller heart. Use a spatula to carefully place cookies on a cookie sheet lined with wax paper leaving an inch between each one as the cookies will expand while baking. Sprinkle the Jolly Rancher candy crumbs in the empty space in the middle of each cookie to fill. Make a variety of colored cookies. Bake in the oven according to the cookie mix instructions until the candies are melted and the cookies are lightly golden brown on the edges. Let cool completely before removing from the pan.

SUPER MOM SAYS: THE DOUGH FOR THESE COOKIES NEEDS TO BE NICE AND FIRM SO THEY WILL HOLD THEIR SHAPE. BE SURE TO ADD ENOUGH EXTRA FLOUR TO THE COOKIE MIX TO CREATE THAT CONSISTENCY. ANOTHER TRICK— DON'T FORGET TO LINE YOUR BAKING SHEET WITH WAX PAPER SO YOUR STAINED GLASS WON'T BECOME A STICKY MESS!

HAPPY HEART
Cookie

Makes 1 large cookie

I remember back in the day making one of these for my high school boyfriend who thought it was the coolest thing ever. Flash forward a few years (or 20), and I still have never had a disappointed recipient.

What You'll Need
- 1 BAG/BOX CHOCOLATE CHIP COOKIE MIX (AND INGREDIENTS REQUIRED PER PACKAGE INSTRUCTIONS—EGG, BUTTER, OR MARGARINE)
- HEART-SHAPED BAKING PAN (YOU CAN USE A ROUND PAN IF YOU DON'T HAVE A HEART SHAPE)
- NON-STICK COOKING SPRAY
- DECORATOR FROSTING AND/OR GEL

Simple Instructions

Preheat the oven per cookie mix instructions. Spray the pan with non-stick cooking spray. In a large bowl, prepare the cookie batter. Spread into the pan and even out with a spatula. Bake according to bar cookie instructions on the package. Once the cookie has cooled completely, use a knife to loosen the edges and then gently remove from the pan. Decorate any way you like with frosting, decorator gel, and sprinkles.

QUALITY TIME WITH THE KIDS: THESE GIANT COOKIES MAKE DELICIOUS AND INEXPENSIVE GIFTS FOR VALENTINE'S DAY OR ANY TIME OF YEAR. I ENJOY HAVING MY KIDS HELP ME DECORATE THEM FOR DAD, GRANDPARENTS, OR FRIENDS AND LETTING THEM USE THE COOKIE AS THEIR CANVAS.

Cranberry Vanilla
SNACK MIX

This party mix is easy to make and perfect to bring to kids' classroom parties. Use seasonal cupcake baking cups to hold individual mini mixes or set up a Valentine's Day snack mix bar and let the kids create their own.

What You'll Need
Use a combination of any of the below ingredients (or whatever you can find in your pantry at home):

- YOGURT PRETZELS
- COCKTAIL PEANUTS
- ALMONDS
- POPCORN
- YOGURT RAISINS
- DRIED CRANBERRIES
- MILK CHOCOLATE CHIPS OR WHITE CHOCOLATE CHIPS
- VALENTINE'S DAY-THEMED PAPER BAKING CUPS

Simple Instructions
Use any combination of the ingredients or add a few of your own to customize. Add a little of each item to each paper baking cup and they are ready to go. This recipe can scale to any number of kids you need to serve.

QUALITY TIME WITH THE KIDS: TO MAKE THIS AN INTERACTIVE SNACK AND INCREASE THE KIDS' INVOLVEMENT, BRING THE INGREDIENTS IN SEPARATE BOWLS AND LET EACH CHILD CUSTOMIZE AND MAKE HIS OWN MIX.

Sweetie
Pie Pops

Makes 8-10

THESE TASTY TREATS ARE SWEET AS PIE AND WHAT KID DOESN'T LOVE FOOD SERVED ON A STICK? YOU'LL BE AMAZED AT HOW QUICKLY THESE HEARTFELT DESSERTS WILL DISAPPEAR AT YOUR NEXT VALENTINE'S DAY PARTY.

What You'll Need

- 2 PACKAGES REFRIGERATED PIE CRUSTS (2 SHEETS PER PACKAGE/4 SHEETS TOTAL)
- 1 CAN CHERRY PIE FILLING (APPROXIMATELY 21 OZ)
- LARGE HEART SHAPED COOKIE CUTTER
- 10 COOKIE POP STICKS
- 1 CONTAINER RED SUGAR SPRINKLES
- 1 TUBE RED DECORATOR GEL (OPTIONAL)
- WHIPPED CREAM OR VANILLA ICE CREAM (OPTIONAL)

Simple Instructions

Preheat oven according to the directions on the pie crust package. Unroll each sheet of pie crust dough onto a clean, flat surface and cut 5-6 hearts out of each sheet (16-20 hearts total). Place half of the hearts on multiple cookie sheets leaving space below each one. Add a small spoonful of cherry pie filling onto the center of each, leaving space around all of the edges. Place a cookie pop stick to cover 1 inch of the bottom point of each heart. Gently place a second heart on top of the first and use a fork to completely seal the entire outside of the pie pop. Sprinkle with red sugar sprinkles if desired. Bake for 12–15 minutes until golden brown. Once cooled, you can add words or designs with decorator gel. Serve with whipped cream or vanilla ice cream.

LEARN FROM MY MISTAKES: GIVE YOURSELF A LITTLE EXTRA TIME ON THESE PRETTY POPS TO MAKE SURE THAT YOU'VE SEALED THEM COMPLETELY. IF NOT, YOU MAY OPEN THE OVEN TO A CHERRY PIE LAVA OOZING OUT THE SIDES.

CELEBRATE SPRINGTIME

Out of the chill of winter appears the promise of spring. Through our children's eyes we see the world in a whole new light and find ourselves re-energized. At least until it comes time to plan the next classroom party, spring carnival, or Easter brunch. *Simply Super Sweets and Treats* to the rescue! Get ready to find your happy place as you hop through the season making Hot Diggety Dog Brownies, delicious Worms & Dirt Pudding Cups, and best of all, Bunny Booty Pancakes. Yes, really!

Critter Country

Colorful, creative, and "oh-so-cute" come to mind when I think of my favorite springtime sweets. From delicious (and nutritious!) grape caterpillars to our bird's nest cookies that make a perfect home for Easter chicks, theses creative critter treats are sure to be a hit at your next garden party or springtime celebration.

Caterpillar Kabobs

Makes 12

Fresh green grapes are the candy of springtime, and these easy-to-make and healthy treats will be a hit with moms and kids alike.

What You'll Need
- 1 LARGE BAG MEDIUM OR LARGE GREEN GRAPES (72+ GRAPES)
- 12 BAMBOO SKEWERS
- 1 CONTAINER WHITE CAKE FROSTING
- 24 CANDY EYES (OR MINI CHOCOLATE CHIPS)

Simple Instructions

Wash and dry grapes completely. It's best to wash them a few hours in advance or the night before so there is no moisture on the grapes. Gently place 6–8 grapes in a row, lengthwise on each bamboo skewer. Lay each skewer flat on a plate or baking sheet so they are horizontal. Using a small knife or toothpick, add a small amount of white cake frosting to the back of each candy eye (or mini chocolate chip) and place them on the top center of the first grape on each skewer to make the face. Do not use decorator gels or tube icings to attach the eyes as they will not stick correctly. Store in a horizontal position in the refrigerator to set.

LEARN FROM MY MISTAKES: AT FIRST GLANCE, THESE LOOK LIKE THE EASIEST "RECIPE" IN THE HISTORY OF . . . . EVER. SUPER MOM CONFESSION: I HAD TO MAKE THESE CRITTERS THREE TIMES UNTIL I FINALLY GOT THEM RIGHT. HERE'S MY LIST OF DON'TS: DON'T USE WET GRAPES (DRY, ROOM TEMPERATURE GRAPES WORK BEST FOR THESE LITTLE GUYS), DON'T TRY TO FREEZE YOUR GRAPES (THEY TURN BROWN AS THEY THAW); DON'T USE DECORATOR GEL IN A TUBE TO ATTACH THE EYES OR THEY WILL SLIDE DOWN THE SIDES OF YOUR CATERPILLAR CUTIE'S FACE.

Springtime
WORMS & DIRT

Makes 12

This gooey, chewy, and muddy mess will delight all the aspiring little gardeners and bug lovers at your next party. And no need to tell them that they are made with fat-free pudding!

What You'll Need

- 12 PRE-PACKAGED FAT-FREE OR SUGAR-FREE CHOCOLATE PUDDING CUPS
- 18–20 OREOS OR SIMILAR CHOCOLATE SANDWICH COOKIES
- 36 GUMMY WORMS
- SPRINGTIME SPRINKLES (FLOWERS, PASTELS, ETC.)

Simple Instructions

Carefully remove the lids from each of the pudding cups, being careful not to leave excess foil on the top. Start by scraping the frosting off of the chocolate cookies. Make "dirt" by placing the cookies in a sealed plastic bag and pounding with a poultry mallet or you can place them in a bowl and mash with a spoon until you have your desired consistency. Add three gummy worms sticking out of each pudding cup, sprinkle cookie crumbs to cover the top of the pudding, and then add springtime sprinkles as desired.

SUPER MOM SAYS: ONE OF MY ORIGINAL FAVORITES, THIS GREAT GROSS-OUT TREAT IS ALWAYS A HIT AT PARTIES AND DOESN'T EVEN INVOLVE TURNING ON AN OVEN. GRAB A FEW READY-MADE INGREDIENTS FROM THE GROCERY STORE AND YOU ARE GOOD TO GO!

Donut Hole
Hedgehogs

Makes 24

THESE DELIGHTFULLY
DARLING HEDGEHOGS ARE
FILLED WITH PERSONALITY
AND ARE A SIMPLE, SWEET
TREAT TO SERVE AT YOUR
NEXT GARDEN PARTY OR
SPRINGTIME CELEBRATION.

What You'll Need
- 1 BAG MINI CHOCOLATE CHIPS
- 2 DOZEN (24) GLAZED DONUT HOLES
- 2 CONTAINERS CHOCOLATE SPRINKLES (JIMMIES)
- BLACK CIRCLE SPRINKLES— USUALLY PART OF A MIX (OPTIONAL)

SUPER MOM SAYS:
SERIOUSLY, THESE HAPPY LITTLE HEDGEHOGS ARE ALMOST TOO CUTE TO EAT. DON'T WORRY ABOUT MAKING EACH FACE IDENTICAL. BY ALLOWING THEM TO BE UNIQUE, THEY WILL SHOWCASE THEIR OWN PERSONALITY.

Simple Instructions

Pour three-quarters of the bag of mini chocolate chips into a microwave-safe bowl. Set the remainder aside as they will be used for the hedgehogs' eyes and noses. Microwave the chocolate chips at 70–80 percent power for 1½–2 minutes stirring every 30 seconds until smooth. Pour the chocolate sprinkles onto a flat plate. Dip three-quarters of each donut hole into the melted chocolate and smooth with a knife. Roll the chocolate-covered side of each donut in the sprinkles until coated. Place a tiny amount of frosting on the back of three mini chocolate chips or black circle sprinkles and apply to the uncovered side of the donut hole to form two eyes and a nose. Place in a single layer on a plate or flat plastic container covered with wax paper. Chill in the refrigerator for 30 minutes to set. Display on a spring-colored plate and serve.

Bright & Beautiful
Butterflies

Makes 12

These beautifully sweet butterflies will be a treat your whole family will enjoy. Dipped in chocolate and coated with bright colors, they'll have your kids buggin' out with excitement.

What You'll Need

- 1 PACKAGE CHOCOLATE CHIPS
  (MILK CHOCOLATE OR SEMI-SWEET)
- 12 PRETZEL RODS
- 24 LARGE PRETZEL TWISTS
- 24 CANDY EYES
- 1 MEDIUM BAG M&M'S OR OTHER
  CANDY-COATED CHOCOLATES
- SPRING COLORED CONFETTI OR
  OTHER SPRINKLES
- WAX PAPER

QUALITY TIME WITH THE KIDS: HAVE YOUR KIDS DECORATE THESE BOLD AND BRIGHT BUTTERFLIES USING THEIR CREATIVE BRAINPOWER. SEE WHAT KIND OF FUN PATTERNS AND COMBINATIONS THEY CAN COME UP WITH!

Simple Instructions

Cover a baking sheet with wax paper. Melt the chocolate chips in the microwave on 70–80 percent power for approximately 1½ minutes until smooth. Stir every 30–45 seconds. First, dip the large pretzel twists completely in the chocolate until covered and place flat on the wax paper in groups of two with the rounded sides of the pretzels facing the left and right and the centers touching. These will become the butterfly's wings. Next, dip the pretzel rods into the melted chocolate and coat two-thirds of the pretzel using a spoon. Smooth off excess. Lay the chocolate covered portion of the pretzel rod vertically on top of the chocolate wings to attach. Add two candy eyes toward the top of the pretzel rod and then place 6–8 of the same color chocolate candies (i.e. all yellow, all orange, etc.) going down the pretzel rod vertically to become the butterfly's body. Add spring colored sprinkles to the wings. Cool in the refrigerator to set completely before removing from wax paper.

CHICKS
on Sticks

Makes 12

IT WOULDN'T BE SPRINGTIME WITHOUT SOME CHEEKY CHICKS. THESE FUN MARSHMALLOW POPS CAN BE MADE IN MINUTES AND DOUBLE AS A DARLING CENTERPIECE.

What You'll Need
- 12 LARGE MARSHMALLOWS
- 12 BAMBOO SKEWERS
- WATER
- 1 CONTAINER YELLOW SUGAR SPRINKLES
- WHITE CAKE FROSTING
- 6 ORANGE M&M'S OR CANDY-COATED CHOCOLATES
- 24 ROUND BLACK SPRINKLES (USUALLY PART OF A MIX) OR BLACK DECORATOR GEL

Simple Instructions

Insert a bamboo skewer into the bottom of each marshmallow. Fill a glass with water and submerge each marshmallow for 5 seconds. Hold the marshmallow over a plate and sprinkle it with the yellow sugar, turning until completely coated. You can also roll the marshmallow in the excess sugar that has fallen onto the plate to complete your coating. Let the marshmallows dry for a few minutes by arranging them vertically in a tall glass. Try to avoid having them touch each other. Cut each of the orange M&M'S in half using a knife. Using a toothpick or a small knife, apply a small amount of white frosting to the flat, chocolate side of the candy and apply horizontally to the middle of the marshmallow as the beak. Apply two black sprinkle eyes above the beak using frosting or draw eyes with black decorator gel. Display in a tall glass.

QUALITY TIME WITH THE KIDS: IF YOU DON'T MIND SOME SUGAR SPRINKLES ENDING UP ON THE FLOOR, THE KIDS WILL LOVE HELPING COAT EACH MARSHMALLOW. YOU MAY WANT TO LEAVE THE FACE DECORATING TO MOM AS IT IS SOMETIMES CHALLENGING FOR LITTLE HANDS TO DO THE SMALL DETAILS.

Bird's Nest
COOKIES

Makes 18–24
Enjoy the delicious side of spring with these colorful cookies that don't require any baking. The chocolate and peanut butter lovers in your life will be chirping for more.

Simple Instructions

Melt the chocolate chips in a microwave-safe container at 70–80 percent power for 1½–2 minutes, stirring every 30 seconds. Once melted and smooth, add the peanut butter and mix until blended. Pour in the entire package of chow mein noodles and stir until coated. Cover a baking pan with wax paper. Drop the mixture by tablespoonfuls onto the wax paper. Press 3–4 robin egg candies into the top of each nest. Let cool in the refrigerator for 30 minutes to 1 hour.

What You'll Need
- 1 PACKAGE (11.5 OZ) SEMI SWEET CHOCOLATE CHIPS
- 3 TABLESPOONS CREAMY PEANUT BUTTER
- 1 PACKAGE (6 OZ) CHOW MEIN NOODLES
- 1 PACKAGE MINI ROBIN EGG CANDIES
- WAX PAPER

SUPER MOM SAYS: THE HARDEST PART OF MAKING THESE COOKIES IS TRYING NOT TO EAT ALL OF THE CHOCOLATE AND PEANUT BUTTER MIXTURE WHILE YOU ARE CREATING THEM . . . YUM! TRY TO LET AT LEAST A FEW OF THEM MAKE IT TO THE PAN.

Ladybug
BITES

Makes 24 cookies

These lovely little ladybugs will put a smile on your kids' faces this spring. They are so simple to make and will add a splash of color to your next garden party or celebration.

What You'll Need
- 1 BOTTLE RED COOKIE ICING
- 24 OREO COOKIES OR OTHER ROUND CHOCOLATE SANDWICH COOKIES
- 48 CANDY EYES
- BLACK CIRCLE SPRINKLES – USUALLY COME IN A MIX (OPTIONAL)
- BLACK DECORATOR GEL

Simple Instructions

If necessary, microwave the cookie icing for 10–15 seconds per package instructions to get to a dispensable consistency. Cover the top of each cookie with red cookie icing, smoothing with a knife if necessary. Place on a plate or tray in the refrigerator to let the frosting harden for 30–45 minutes. After the icing has set, apply two candy eyes close together on the front of each cookie. Apply 8–10 black circle sprinkles over the rest of the red icing for the ladybug's spots. You can also create the spots with black decorator gel if you don't have black circle sprinkles. Use the black decorator gel to draw a vertical line from the top of the cookie almost down to the eyes and then create a small "y" shape by making short lines to the left and right over the eyes to create the wings.

SUPER MOM SAYS: WHEN YOU ARE MAKING THESE LITTLE LADIES, BE SURE TO PUT THEM ON A PLATE OR PAPER TOWEL WHILE YOU ARE COATING THEM WITH FROSTING. YOU MAY ALSO WANT TO WEAR AN APRON OR CHANGE INTO YOUR "NOT-SO-NICE" CLOTHES. THE RED COOKIE ICING MAKES A COLORFUL IMPACT BUT IT ALSO TENDS TO GET ALL OVER THE PLACE.

A Playful St. Patty's Day

The luck of the Irish will be with you this year when you magically make these treats that are definitely easier than catching a leprechaun.

Pot-of-Gold
Party Fruit

Serves 8-12

THIS DELICIOUS AND NUTRITIOUS RECIPE MAKES A GREAT ADDITION TO EVERY ST. PATTY'S DAY PARTY OR ANYTIME YOU ARE LOOKING TO ADD A BURST OF COLOR TO ONE OF YOUR CELEBRATIONS.

What You'll Need

- 1 SMALL CONTAINER STRAWBERRIES – SLICED
- 1 CAN MANDARIN ORANGES OR 4–5 FRESH MANDARIN ORANGES – PEELED AND IN SECTIONS
- 1 CAN PINEAPPLE CHUNKS
- 1 BAG GREEN GRAPES
- 1 MEDIUM CONTAINER BLUEBERRIES
- 1 CONTAINER WHIPPED TOPPING (OR 1 CUP MINI MARSHMALLOWS)
- 10–20 GOLD FOIL-COVERED CHOCOLATE COINS OR ROLO CHOCOLATE CARAMEL CANDIES STILL WRAPPED

SUPER MOM SAYS: DEPENDING ON THE TIME OF YEAR, YOU MAY NOT HAVE ACCESS TO FRESH FRUIT FOR EACH OF THE LAYERS OF THE RAINBOW. FEEL FREE TO USE CANNED OR FROZEN FRUIT AS NEEDED. YOU CAN ALSO SUBSTITUTE SIMILAR COLORED FRUIT SUCH AS BANANAS INSTEAD OF PINEAPPLE, OR KIWIS INSTEAD OF GREEN GRAPES. MIX THINGS UP!

Simple Instructions

Start by washing the strawberries, removing the stems, and then slicing vertically. Set aside. If using fresh mandarin oranges, peel and then separate into sections. Pineapple chunks are definitely easier to use straight out of the can as they are ready to go. Simply drain the excess juice and set aside. Thoroughly wash the green grapes and blueberries and dry on a paper towel to remove excess water. Once all the fruit is prepared, arrange on a large platter creating the arcs of a rainbow from largest to smallest—red, orange, yellow, green, and blue. Add whipped topping or mini marshmallows in a small bowl on the left to form a cloud and then place a handful of chocolate gold coins or ROLO candies on the right as the "pot of gold."

Sweet & Salty

SHAMROCKS

Makes 24

You'll be feeling very lucky as you make these simple snacks, which take only minutes instead of hours. No baking required!

What You'll Need

- 24 MINI TWIST PRETZELS
- 72 GREEN M&M'S OR CANDY-COATED CHOCOLATES
- 1 CONTAINER CHOCOLATE CAKE FROSTING
- WHITE DECORATOR ICING IN TUBE OR AEROSOL CAN

Simple Instructions

Arrange pretzels on a tray or plate in an upside down position (single point on top). Apply the chocolate frosting to each pretzel so it is covering each of the three holes. Gently apply one green candy to each hole. Using white decorator icing, draw a line on each shamrock from the top middle of the green candy down to the bottom of the pretzel to resemble a stem. Store them in an airtight container in the refrigerator until set.

LEARN FROM MY MISTAKES: AS SIMPLE AS THESE LITTLE GUYS ARE TO MAKE, I ACTUALLY BLEW IT THE FIRST TIME AROUND. BE SURE TO USE CHOCOLATE FROSTING UNDER THE GREEN CANDIES AS WHITE FROSTING DOESN'T LOOK AS GOOD. ALSO, STEER CLEAR OF WHITE DECORATOR GEL AS IT COMES OUT ALMOST CLEAR. WHITE CUPCAKE ICING IN A DISPENSER CAN OR OPAQUE DECORATOR FROSTING WORK BEST.

Egg-ceptional Easter Treats

Easter will always hold a special place in my heart. My husband proposed to me on Easter with my engagement ring in a big, plastic, purple egg. Very creative! My first born, Morgan, decided to make her grand entrance into the world, also on Easter. Hey . . . that's one way to get out of cooking Easter dinner! Throughout history, Easter has always been a time for new beginnings. As busy moms, it's time to jump on that band wagon and begin to see that semi-homemade treats can definitely save our sanity!

BUNNY BOOTY
Pancakes

Number of servings varies.

THESE ADORABLE SPRINGTIME PANCAKES ARE SURE TO PUT A HOP IN YOUR KIDS' STEP. SURPRISE THEM ON EASTER MORNING WITH THIS BOOTY-LICIOUS BREAKFAST TREAT.

What You'll Need

- PANCAKE MIX
- WATER
- NON-STICK COOKING SPRAY
- FRESH STRAWBERRIES
- PINK SPRINKLES
- WHIPPED CREAM IN A CAN

Simple Instructions

Preheat a large skillet on the stove according to pancake mix instructions. Prepare the amount of pancake batter you need according to package directions. Using a small measuring cup, pour 3 pancakes into the pan—1 medium-sized circle and 2 smaller oval-shaped pancakes. After 1–1½ minutes, flip the pancakes and cook for another 1–1½ minutes. Using a spatula, remove when completely cooked and lightly browned on each side. Place the larger circle-shaped pancake in the center of a plate and then put one of the oval pancakes overlapping the lower left side and one on the lower right side at an angle (these will be the bunny's feet). Slice strawberries and place one slice in the center of each foot. Put three pink sprinkles vertically on the bottom of each foot to make paws. Spray whipped cream in the center of the larger pancake to make the tail.

SUPER MOM SAYS: THIS SUPER CUTE BREAKFAST WILL HAVE YOUR KIDS THINKING THAT YOU ARE "THE BEST MOM EVER" WHEN IN FACT, THESE ARE THE EXACT SAME INGREDIENTS YOU WOULD HAVE LIKELY USED FOR REGULAR PANCAKES. IT'S AMAZING WHAT A LITTLE KITCHEN CREATIVITY CAN DO!

Easy Easter
CUPCAKES

Makes 18-24 cupcakes
These cupcakes are easy to make and an egg-citing Easter activity to create with the kids. They will come hopping back for more once they taste these easy Easter goodies.

What You'll Need
- 1 BOX CAKE MIX (FLAVOR OF YOUR CHOICE—I LIKE LEMON OR STRAWBERRY FOR SPRING)
- INGREDIENTS TO PREPARE CAKE MIX (I.E. EGGS, OIL, WATER)
- 24 PAPER CUPCAKE BAKING CUPS IN PASTEL COLORS
- GREEN CUPCAKE ICING IN A CAN WITH TIPS INCLUDED
- 24 PEEPS MARSHMALLOW BUNNIES (VARIOUS COLORS)
- 1 BAG MINI ROBIN EGG CANDIES

Simple Instructions

Preheat the oven and prepare cake mix according to package instructions for cupcakes. Line the cupcake pan with paper baking cups and fill each ⅔ full with batter. Bake according to package directions. Remove the cupcakes from the pan and cool completely before decorating. Attach the star tip to the can of green cupcake icing and use quick pulses to apply the frosting to the top of each cupcake to look like grass. Cut ¼ inch off the bottom of each Peeps marshmallow bunny so the bottom is flat, and then place on top of each frosted cupcake. Decorate with 2–3 robin eggs.

SUPER MOM SAYS: I AM A HUGE FAN OF THE CAKE AND CUPCAKE ICING IN AEROSOL CANS. IT IS SO CONVENIENT BECAUSE IT COMES IN MANY COLORS AND INCLUDES A VARIETY OF TIPS. THERE ARE MULTIPLE COMPANIES THAT MAKE IT (BETTY CROCKER AND WILTON ARE A FEW OF MY FAVORITES), SO TAKE YOUR PICK. YOU DON'T NEED TO BE A PROFESSIONAL BAKER TO MAKE YOUR CUPCAKES LOOK LIKE A MILLION BUCKS!

Egg-ceptional Cereal Treats

Makes 12-18 large eggs, or 18-24 small eggs

A COLORFUL AND SEASONAL TWIST ON THE MARSHMALLOW CRISPY TREATS WE ALL LOVE. THIS EASY EASTER RECIPE FOR KIDS IS A FUN WAY TO CELEBRATE SPRING AND ALL ITS FRESH COLORS.

What You'll Need

- ½ CUP BUTTER OR MARGARINE
- 1 BAG (10 OZ) MINI MARSHMALLOWS
- 8½ CUPS FRUITY PEBBLES CEREAL OR OTHER COLORFUL PUFFED RICE CEREAL
- 12-18 LARGE PLASTIC EGGS, OR 24 SMALL PLASTIC EGGS

LEARN FROM MY MISTAKES: BE SURE TO LET THESE GOODIES SET COMPLETELY BEFORE TRYING TO CRACK THEM OPEN. IF YOU OPEN TOO EARLY, YOU'LL END UP WITH A GOOEY, STICKY MESS!

Simple Instructions

Melt the butter in a microwave-safe mixing bowl for 30–45 seconds. Add the mini marshmallows and stir to coat. Microwave the marshmallow mixture for 1–2 minutes, stirring every 45 seconds. Once melted and smooth, add the cereal and stir until coated completely. Spray the inside of the plastic eggs with cooking spray to prevent sticking. Fill each half of the plastic egg with cereal mix and then close. Let them set for at least one hour before opening the eggs.

Plastic Egg
PARTY MIX

Recycle and reuse your egg cartons for this kid-friendly party mix. Other moms will applaud your resourcefulness and the kids will enjoy creating their own combination of treats.

What You'll Need

- EMPTY EGG CARTONS (DOZEN-EGG SIZE), CUT IN HALF
- 6 MEDIUM PLASTIC EGGS PER HALF CARTON
- POPCORN
- CHOCOLATE CHIPS
- MINI MARSHMALLOWS
- PASTEL M&M'S OR ROBIN EGG CANDIES
- YOGURT PRETZELS
- CEREAL
- PEANUTS
- ANY OTHER SNACK MIX INGREDIENTS

Simple Instructions

Cut each egg carton in half so there are 6 egg holders in each container. Each egg carton will make two treat containers. Insert 6 plastic eggs (a variety of colors) into the cups. Open each egg but leave the tops attached. Create a treat buffet that has large bowls of each individual snack item. Let each child go through the line and select items to fills each of their 6 plastic eggs. Scale to the number of children being served.

SUPER MOM SAYS: IF YOU ARE BRINGING THIS TREAT TO A CLASSROOM PARTY, BE SURE TO CHECK WITH YOUR CHILD'S TEACHER TO SEE IF THERE ARE ANY ALLERGIES. INCLUDE SNACK ITEMS THAT CAN BE ENJOYED BY ALL MEMBERS OF THE CLASS.

Egg Hunt
Brownies

Makes 18–24 brownies

THE KIDS WILL BE RACING
TO THE DESSERT TABLE WHEN
THEY SEE THESE CHEWY
CHOCOLATE TREATS. SERVE
THEM ON A FESTIVE PASTEL-
COLORED PLATE AND YOU'LL
HAVE THE PERFECT ADDITION
TO ANY EASTER GATHERING.

What You'll Need
- 1 PACKAGE BROWNIE MIX
- INGREDIENTS TO PREPARE
  BROWNIES (I.E. OIL, EGGS,
  WATER)
- 1 CAN GREEN CUPCAKE ICING
  WITH TIPS INCLUDED
- 1 BAG PASTEL PEANUT M&M'S
  OR ROBIN EGG CANDIES
- NON-STICK COOKING SPRAY
- 9 X 12-INCH BAKING PAN

Simple Instructions

Preheat the oven and prepare the brownie batter in a large bowl according to the brownie mix instructions. Coat the bottom and sides of a 9 x 12-inch baking pan with non-stick cooking spray then pour the batter into the pan. Smooth the top with a spatula. Bake according to package instructions. Remove from the oven and let cool completely. Cut the brownies into the desired size (approximately 2" x 2"), remove from the pan, and place on a plate. Attach the star tip to the green cupcake frosting, and using quick pulses, apply to the entire top of each brownie to create grass. Apply 3 M&M'S or robin egg candies to decorate.

QUALITY TIME WITH THE
KIDS: GETTING THE KIDS
INTO THE KITCHEN IS A
WAY TO CREATE LASTING
LIFETIME MEMORIES. MY
CHILDREN LOVE BAKING
AND A RECIPE LIKE THIS IS
THE PERFECT WAY TO GET
THEM INVOLVED.

Mom Rocks and Dads & Grads Are on a Roll

As moms, we are the queens of our castles, the keepers of family calendars, and the kids' confidants. It may not be often, but at least on Mother's Day maybe Dad and the kids can make a few of these tasty treats to celebrate *our* special day. Hint: Leave this book open to the page with the treat you'd like them to make!

And for our dynamite dads, Mom is sure to score big when you whip up these easy sports-themed snacks just for him on Father's Day. Got some graduates in your house? Celebrate their rite of passage with simple sweets that double as cute centerpieces.

MOTHER'S DAY
Micro Mini's

Make Mom's day with these mini Mother's Day cookie pops the kids can decorate with love.
Bundle them together to make a micro-bouquet or use at the table for each guest's place card.

What You'll Need

- MINI SPRING-SHAPED COOKIE CUTTERS (FLOWER, TULIP, BUTTERFLY, HEART), YOU CAN PICK THESE UP AT A CRAFT STORE USUALLY IN A SET
- 1 BAG PACKAGED SUGAR COOKIE MIX
- INGREDIENTS TO PREPARE COOKIE MIX PER PACKAGE INSTRUCTIONS (I.E. 1 STICK BUTTER; 1 EGG)
- FLOUR
- COLORED TOOTHPICKS
- FROSTING & DECORATOR GEL, VARIOUS COLORS (OPTIONAL)
- SPRINKLES, SPRINGTIME COLORS AND SHAPES
- BAKING SHEET

Simple Instructions

Preheat the oven per cookie mix instructions. Prepare the cookie dough as indicated on the package for cutout cookies. Use extra flour as necessary so the dough is not too sticky. Flour a clean, dry surface and roll out cookie dough to approximately ¼ inch thick. Press each cookie cutter into the dough and trim off the edges.

Transfer to a cookie sheet using a spatula. Leave at least ½–1 inch between each cookie as they will expand when baking. Gently insert a toothpick into the bottom of each one, being careful not to alter the shape. These are easier to decorate with sprinkles before you put them in the oven since they are so small. Bake according to package instructions, but check a few minutes earlier since the cookies are small and may be ready sooner. They should be just slightly golden brown on the edges. Let cool on a baking sheet for 2 minutes and then gently place on aluminum foil. If you are decorating with gel, frosting, and sprinkles, do so once cookies are completely cooled.

SUPER MOM SAYS: THERE'S SOMETHING ABOUT MAKING THINGS "MINI" THAT JUST ADDS A FUN FACTOR TO THIS RECIPE. I RECEIVED SO MANY COMPLIMENTS WHEN I MADE THESE LAST TIME INCLUDING: "THESE ARE SOOOOO CUTE!" "ADORABLE!" AND "I'M GOING TO MAKE THESE FOR MY NEXT PARTY!"

MOM'S THE BOMB BREAKFAST BRUSCHETTA

Makes 8–12 slices

Looking for an easy recipe for Mother's Day brunch? These four-ingredient breakfast bruschettas are so easy even the kids can make them—with as little help from Dad!

What You'll Need

- 4–6 SLICES CINNAMON RAISIN BREAD
- WHIPPED PLAIN CREAM CHEESE
- SLICED STRAWBERRIES
- BLUEBERRIES (TO GARNISH)

QUALITY TIME WITH THE KIDS: SINCE IT IS MOTHER'S DAY AFTER ALL, THIS IS DAD'S TIME TO ENJOY MAKING BREAKFAST WITH THE KIDS. IF YOUR CHILDREN ARE OLDER, THEY MAY EVEN BE ABLE TO MAKE THESE ALL ON THEIR OWN SINCE THERE IS NO BAKING INVOLVED.

Simple Instructions

Toast the cinnamon raisin bread in the toaster until lightly browned. Wash, dry, and cut the strawberries vertically into multiple slices. Once the bread is toasted, cut each piece in half and trim off the crust if desired. You will end up with two rectangular pieces from each slice of toast. Spread with cream cheese and top with fresh strawberries. Garnish with blueberries and other fruit. Delicious!

BATTER UP BITES

Makes 24 cookies

You'll hit a home run after the baseball game or with Dad on Father's Day when you make these simple, three-ingredient sweet treats.

What You'll Need

- 24 OREO COOKIES, OR OTHER ROUND CHOCOLATE SANDWICH COOKIES
- 1 BOTTLE WHITE COOKIE ICING
- RED DECORATOR ICING IN A TUBE
- RED SPRINKLES (OPTIONAL)

LEARN FROM MY MISTAKES: THIS RECIPE IS ALMOST FOOL-PROOF AS LONG AS YOU USE THE CORRECT INGREDIENTS AND HAVE A STEADY HAND. I DON'T RECOMMEND USING CAKE FROSTING TO COAT THE COOKIES SINCE IT ISN'T AS SMOOTH. I FOUND THAT USING OPAQUE RED DECORATOR ICING SHOWS UP MUCH BETTER THAN THE DECORATOR GEL, WHICH DOESN'T CREATE QUITE AS STRONG OF A COLOR IMPACT.

Simple Instructions

If necessary, microwave the cookie icing for 10–15 seconds per package instructions to get a pourable consistency. Cover the top of each cookie with white cookie icing. Smooth with a knife if necessary. Place on a plate or tray in the refrigerator to let the frosting harden for 30 minutes. After the icing has set, draw a half circle facing inward on each side of the cookie with red decorator icing. Draw 3–4 small perpendicular lines on each semicircle to look like baseball stitching. You can also use red sprinkles (small lines) for the stitching if you prefer.

Hole-in-One
Brownies

Makes 12

These par-fect little brownie bites are fun for Father's Day or after a round of golf. They are so easy to make, you can whip up a dozen or two in a matter of minutes.

What You'll Need

- 12 PRE-MADE CIRCULAR MINI-BROWNIES FROM THE BAKERY (YOU CAN ALSO MAKE YOUR OWN BROWNIES IF YOU PREFER)
- 1 CAN GREEN CUPCAKE ICING WITH DECORATOR TIPS (USE THE STAR TIP TO MAKE GRASS)
- 12 WHITE CIRCLE SPRINKLES (THESE USUALLY COME IN A MIX WITH ASSORTED COLORS), OR PEARL SPRINKLES
- COLORED TOOTHPICKS
- CONSTRUCTION PAPER (VARIOUS COLORS)
- GLUE STICK

SUPER MOM SAYS:
CUPCAKE ICING IN A CAN IS ONE OF MY FAVORITE SUPER MOM SECRETS. A PIECE OF ADVICE—SINCE THE FROSTING IS UNDER PRESSURE, BE SURE TO TEST A BIT ON A PAPER TOWEL BEFORE YOU START APPLYING TO YOUR BROWNIES. SOMETIMES IT TAKES A FEW SQUIRTS BEFORE THE CONSISTENCY IS CORRECT AND YOU GET THE HANG OF THE APPLICATION.

Simple Instructions

Attach the star tip to the green cupcake icing. Remove the brownies from their package and one at a time cover the top of each brownie with green "grass" by applying the icing in small pulses in a circular motion. While you are frosting the brownies, have your kids cut small triangles out of a variety of colored paper and glue to the toothpicks to make the golf flags. Stick the toothpick flags into the frosted brownies and add a white circular sprinkle on top of the green frosting for the ball.

Choco
Grad Caps

Makes 12

GRADUATION IS SWEET . . .
AND SO ARE THESE
ADORABLE CHOCOLATE
GRADUATION CAPS! SERVE
AS A DESSERT OR ADD TO
A FLORAL CENTERPIECE AT
YOUR GRAD'S CELEBRA-
TION.

What You'll Need
- 12 MILK CHOCOLATE SQUARES
  (WE USED GHIRARDELLI)
- 12 REESE'S PEANUT BUTTER CUP
  MINIS
- CHOCOLATE CAKE FROSTING
  OR MELTED CHOCOLATE CHIPS
- YELLOW DECORATOR ICING
- 12 BAMBOO SKEWERS
  (OPTIONAL)

SUPER MOM SAYS:
THESE CUTE CAPS WILL
BE A GREAT ADDITION
TO YOUR GRADUATION
PARTY DÉCOR AND
CAN ALSO BE A CLEVER
"CONGRATULATIONS"
GIFT FOR A FRIEND OR
FAMILY MEMBER WHO IS
CELEBRATING HIS OR HER
SCHOOL SUCCESS.

Simple Instructions
Unwrap the chocolate squares and Reese's Peanut Butter Cup Minis. Put a small
amount of frosting or melted chocolate chips on the smaller side of the Reese's cup
and attach to the center of the chocolate square. Draw a diagonal line from the
center of the square out to the corner and dripping down the side to make a tassel.
Cool in the refrigerator. Add a skewer to the bottom if desired, and display.

SUMMER FUN

School's out . . . sizzle, splash, summertime! The long-awaited summer break is here . . . so why are you already so stressed out? Moms don't really get a "vacation" since we are typically working harder than ever. Give yourself a break when it comes to your party prep by trying some of these recipes that are as easy as a summer breeze. Whether you are feeling patriotic or just in the mood to be a beach bum, these sunny sweets will bring a smile to your face.

Simply, Super Summer

Backyard barbecues, trips to the beach, and long summer road trips share one thing in common . . . snacks! Whip up these super easy sunshine-filled treats, which only require a few ingredients. Your family will be screaming for s'more!

Fun Flip-Flop Cookies

What You'll Need

- 24 NUTTER BUTTER
  COOKIES
- DECORATOR ICING TUBES
  IN MULTIPLE COLORS OF
  YOUR CHOICE
- FLOWER-SHAPED
  SPRINKLES (OPTIONAL)

SUPER MOM SAYS: THESE
ARE THE PERFECT TREAT
TO BRING TO A PARTY
IN A PINCH. KEEP A BAG
OF NUTTER BUTTERS IN
YOUR PANTRY ALONG
WITH MULTI-COLORED
DECORATOR ICINGS AND
GET READY TO BE THE HIT
OF YOUR NEXT BEACH
BASH!

Simple Instructions

Place cookies on a serving plate or tray and one by one add the straps of the
flip-flop by piping an upside-down, curved "V" shape on one side of the cookie
(point at the top). Use a variety of colors to make your plate look festive. Add a
complementary colored flower sprinkle at the center of the "V" to make your flip-flops
fashionable. Allow the frosting to set before serving.

BITE-SIZED
Banana Splits

Makes 12

WHO DOESN'T LOVE A DELICIOUS BANANA SPLIT ON A HOT SUMMER DAY? MAKE YOUR TROUBLES MELT AWAY WHEN YOU NIBBLE ON THESE BITE-SIZED SWEETS ON A STICK.

What You'll Need

- 6 MEDIUM TO LARGE STRAWBERRIES
- 2 MEDIUM TO LARGE BANANAS
- 1 CONTAINER VANILLA ICE CREAM (OR FLAVOR OF YOUR CHOICE)
- 12 MARASCHINO CHERRIES
- 1 BOTTLE CHOCOLATE SYRUP, COLD
- COLORED SPRINKLES
- 6 BAMBOO KABOB SKEWERS, OR 12 COOKIE POP STICKS
- MELON BALL SCOOP
- WAX PAPER

Simple Instructions

Cut bamboo skewers in half so there are 12 pieces. Wash and dry the strawberries. Remove the stems and slice each strawberry vertically into 2 equal pieces. Peel the bananas and cut them into 12 one-inch pieces. Using the melon ball tool in a twisting motion, scoop 12 mini ice cream balls out of the container. Immediately stack the fruit and ice cream on each stick—strawberry, ice cream ball, banana, and cherry on top. Place flat on a plate covered with wax paper. Drizzle the refrigerated chocolate syrup on top of the ice cream and fruit. Add colored sprinkles if desired and place immediately in the freezer to set.

QUALITY TIME WITH THE KIDS: ON SIZZLING HOT SUMMER DAYS, THIS CAN BE AN EXCITING INDOOR ACTIVITY THAT WILL HELP THE KIDS KEEP THEIR COOL. OF COURSE, WHEN IT COMES TIME TO EAT THESE MINI MORSELS, SEND THEM BACK OUTSIDE TO AVOID A MELTED MESS!

S'mores on a Stick

Makes 12

These are a family camping tradition made easy. S'mores on a Stick have the same great taste without the use of a campfire. Don't be surprised when the kids come back asking for s'more.

What You'll Need

- 1 BOX HONEY GRAHAM CRACKERS
- 12 LARGE MARSHMALLOWS
- 24 HERSHEY'S KISSES
- 12 BAMBOO SKEWERS

LEARN FROM MY MISTAKES: THE TRICK TO GETTING THESE S'MORES JUST RIGHT IS THE MELTING OF THE CHOCOLATE. IF YOU OVER-MELT, THEY WILL BECOME TOO GOOPY. UNDER-MELT, AND THEY WON'T STICK TO THE MARSHMALLOW. A GOOD TEST IS TO CAREFULLY PRESS DOWN ON THE TOP OF ONE OF THE KISSES WHILE THEY ARE IN THE OVEN. IF THE TOP EASILY COMPRESSES WHILE THE REST STILL HOLDS ITS SHAPE AND FEELS SOFT TO THE TOUCH, THEY ARE READY TO GO.

Simple Instructions

Preheat the oven to 275°F. Break graham crackers into fourths so you have 24 rectangles, and lay them flat on a cookie sheet. Unwrap the Hershey's Kisses and place two on each graham cracker. Place in the oven for 10 minutes so the Kisses soften but are not completely melted.

While they are in the oven, use a knife to cut each marshmallow horizontally in half so they look like a circle. Stack both pieces of marshmallow vertically on top of each other on the kabob sticks so the flat circles of the marshmallows are facing the sides. Remove the chocolate graham crackers from the oven and press a marshmallow kabob onto half of them.

Top each kabob with the remaining chocolate graham crackers with the chocolate facing the marshmallows. Serving these warm is preferred, but they can also be eaten at room temperature.

HOT DIGGETY DOG
Brownies

Makes 18–24

INSPIRED BY SUMMER BACKYARD BARBECUES, THESE GRILL-TASTIC GOODIES ARE FUN TO MAKE FOR ANY OUTDOOR EVENT.

What You'll Need

- 1 BAG OR BOX OF BROWNIE MIX
- NECESSARY INGREDIENTS TO PREPARE (EGGS, OIL, WATER, ETC.)
- HOT TAMALES CANDIES
- WHITE DECORATOR ICING
- 1 CONTAINER CHOCOLATE CAKE FROSTING
- ORANGE SUGAR SPRINKLES
- CUPCAKE PAN
- 24 SILVER CUPCAKE BAKING CUPS

Simple Instructions

Preheat the oven and prepare the brownie mix in a large bowl according to the directions on the box. Line the cupcake pan with silver baking cups. Pour the batter into each cup, about two-thirds full, and bake according to package directions. Cool completely. To decorate, use the white decorator icing and make 4–5 "grill lines" across the top of each brownie. Apply orange sugar sprinkles to the top of each one. Use a dinner knife or toothpick dipped in chocolate frosting to make 3–4 "grill lines" on top of each of the Hot Tamales candies. Place 3 Hot Tamales candies on each brownie to make hot dogs.

SUPER MOM SAYS: IF YOU ARE MAKING THESE FOR A SPECIAL OCCASION, BE SURE TO PUT A "DO NOT EAT" SIGN ON TOP. I WAS PREPARING THESE FOR A BIG TV APPEARANCE LAST YEAR AND WHEN I WENT TO THE REFRIGERATOR TO GRAB THEM, HALF OF THEM WERE EATEN BY MY HUSBAND AND KIDS. THEY ARE JUST TOO CUTE TO RESIST!

SUMMER ICE CREAM SANDWICHES

These sunshine-filled sweets will cool your kids off during the dog days of summer. A fun alternative to cupcakes or cookies, serve these frozen treats at your next summer celebration and customize with seasonal sprinkles.

What You'll Need

- 8 ICE CREAM SANDWICHES, VANILLA OR CHOCOLATE
- SEASONAL SUMMER-COLORED SPRINKLES

QUALITY TIME WITH THE KIDS: IF YOU CAN KEEP THE KIDS FROM LICKING THEIR FINGERS, THIS IS A SIMPLE RECIPE THAT WILL ALLOW EVEN THE LITTLE ONES TO HELP IN THE KITCHEN. TRY A TWIST ON THESE DURING THE FALL AND MAKE MAKING ICE-SCREAM SANDWICHES FOR HALLOWEEN.

Simple Instructions

Unwrap the ice cream sandwiches and cut each into two equal sections so you have 16 pieces. Pour the sprinkles onto a plate and coat all four sides of each ice cream sandwich. Place in an airtight container and re-freeze to set until ready to serve.

Beachy Keen Cupcakes

Makes 24 cupcakes

Get ready for some fun in the sun with these beach-themed cupcakes. Perfect for summer celebrations, birthday parties, or a backyard barbecue!

What You'll Need

- 1 BOX CUPCAKE MIX, FLAVOR OF YOUR CHOICE
- INGREDIENTS TO PREPARE CAKE MIX (EGGS, WATER, ETC.)
- 24 SILVER OR BLUE CUPCAKE BAKING CUPS
- 1 CAN LIGHT BLUE DECORATOR CUPCAKE ICING WITH STAR DECORATING TIP
- 12 MINI NILLA WAFERS COOKIES
- PEPPERIDGE FARM GOLDFISH SNACK CRACKERS (SWEET FLAVORS PREFERRED)
- DECORATOR ICING IN PRIMARY COLORS (RED, YELLOW, BLUE, GREEN)

SUPER MOM SAYS: THE CUTE LITTLE BEACH BALL COOKIES USED AS DECORATIONS FOR THIS RECIPE CAN ALSO BE SERVED ON THEIR OWN. DISPLAY ON A SUMMER-THEMED PLATTER AND YOU'VE GOT AN EASY ADDITION TO YOUR NEXT BEACH EXTRAVAGANZA.

Simple Instructions

Preheat the oven according to package instructions and line the cupcake pan with paper baking cups. In a large mixing bowl, prepare the cupcake mix, fill each baking cup ⅔ full with batter, and bake according to directions.

While the cupcakes are baking, use colored frostings (red, yellow, blue) to make beach balls with the Nilla Wafers (one color in the center and different colors on each side). Be sure to let the frosting set. Add blue or green frosting eyes to 24 of the goldfish. Once the cupcakes are baked, let them cool and frost them using the canned light blue frosting with the star tip. Apply using small pulses to distribute the frosting on top of each cupcake. Decorate half of the cupcakes with beach balls and half with two goldfish.

TROPICAL FRUIT TOWER

Don't tell the kids, but this delicious dessert is actually good for them. Use the freshest fruit from the season, layer on the flavors of summer, and top with a touch of whipped cream and a beach umbrella. Sun-sational!

What You'll Need

- 1 SMALL CONTAINER STRAWBERRIES, SLICED
- 1 CAN MANDARIN ORANGES, OR PEACHES
- 1 CAN PINEAPPLE CHUNKS
- 1 BAG GREEN GRAPES
- 1 MEDIUM CONTAINER BLUEBERRIES
- 1 SMALL CONTAINER RASPBERRIES (OPTIONAL)
- 1 CONTAINER WHIPPED TOPPING, OR 1 CUP MINI MARSHMALLOWS
- 4 TALL, CLEAR CUPS, OR GLASSES
- 4 PAPER UMBRELLAS

Simple Instructions

Start by washing and drying all the fresh fruit. You can use the suggested types of fruit or pick your own seasonal fruit. Remove strawberry stems and slice vertically into multiple pieces. Remove grapes from the vine. For any canned fruit, open and drain excess juice. Once all the fruit is prepared, layer small amounts of each fruit in the glasses, top with whipped cream, a raspberry, and a tropical umbrella.

SUPER MOM SAYS: THIS IS A FANTASTIC WAY TO GET YOUR KIDS TO EAT THEIR FRUIT. IT'S BOTH FANCY AND FUN AND WHO DOESN'T ENJOY BEING SERVED A DESSERT WITH AN UMBRELLA ON TOP?

Makes 24

ICE CREAM COOKIE CONES

Heading to a summer picnic and need to bring a convenient yet creative dessert? These "ice cream" cookie cones will be a festive addition to your gathering without having you lose your cool while you prepare them.

What You'll Need
- 24 NUTTER BUTTER COOKIES
- 2 CUPS WHITE CANDY MELTS, OR WHITE CHOCOLATE BAKING CHIPS
- 1 TABLESPOON SHORTENING (OPTIONAL)
- 24 CINNAMON DROP CANDIES OR RED M&M'S CHOCOLATE CANDIES OR OTHER CANDY-COATED CHOCOLATES
- COLORED SPRINKLES SUCH AS RAINBOW NONPAREILS
- WAX PAPER

Simple Instructions
In a microwave-safe container, melt the white chocolate baking chips or candy melts at 50–60 percent power, stirring every 30 seconds. Be careful not to overheat as the white chocolate can seize up. If the mixture is a little too thick, add a tablespoon of shortening and stir to the desired consistency. Spoon the melted white chocolate over the top third of each Nutter Butter in a circular shape to look like a scoop of ice cream. Place flat on a baking sheet or tray covered with wax paper. Repeat for all the cookies. Sprinkle with the rainbow nonpareils to decorate, and add a red candy at the top as the "cherry." Place in the refrigerator to set.

SUPER MOM SAYS: THESE TOTALLY EASY TREATS WILL ADD A LITTLE SUNSHINE TO EVERY SUMMER TABLE. IF YOU HAVE TIME, TRY USING PINK AND BROWN CANDY MELTS IN ADDITION TO THE WHITE SO YOUR PLATTER WILL HAVE "CHOCOLATE, STRAWBERRY, AND VANILLA" CONES.

Beach
Buckets

Makes 4

Nothing says summer like a day at the beach. If you don't have an ocean nearby, these little blue beauties will help your kids feel like they are catching a California wave.

What You'll Need

- 1 CONTAINER JELL-O BRAND BERRY BLUE GELATIN
- HOT WATER
- 12 GUMMY FISH CANDIES
- 4 SMALL CLEAR PLASTIC CUPS
- 4 WHOLE GRAHAM CRACKERS
- 4 PAPER UMBRELLAS (OPTIONAL)

LEARN FROM MY MISTAKES: BE SURE TO ALLOW THE JELL-O TO SET FOR 15–20 MINUTES BEFORE YOU ADD THE GUMMY FISH. IF YOU ADD THEM IMMEDIATELY THEY WILL SINK INSTEAD OF SWIM.

Simple Instructions

Prepare JELL-O according to the directions on the package. Pour equal amounts into 4 clear plastic cups and place in the refrigerator for about 15–20 minutes. When it starts to slightly gel, remove the cups and insert 3 gummy fish into each one. Place back into the refrigerator until completely set.

Place the graham crackers into a plastic bag and seal. Pound the crackers with a mallet or hard object to make crumbs, which will be the "sand" on top of your blue "ocean." Remove the JELL-O from the refrigerator and cover the top with the graham cracker crumbs. Insert an umbrella and serve.

Summer Sweet Scoops

Makes 12 treats

SHOW YOUR LOVE SCOOP BY SCOOP
WITH THESE SUMMER SWEET SCOOPS
CONES. KIDS WILL BE WOWED BY
THE ICE CREAM CONE SHAPE THAT
IS A FUN TWIST ON THE TRADITIONAL
MARSHMALLOW CEREAL TREATS
FROM OUR CHILDHOODS.

What You'll Need

- 1 BAG LARGE MARSHMALLOWS,
  OR 4 CUPS MINI MARSHMALLOWS
- 6 CUPS COLORFUL CEREAL OF
  YOUR CHOICE (FROOT LOOPS,
  TRIX, ETC.)
- 3 TABLESPOONS BUTTER OR
  MARGARINE
- 12 SUGAR CONES
- WAX PAPER
- NON-STICK COOKING SPRAY

LEARN FROM MY MISTAKES:
YES, THESE GOODIES ARE
CUTE BUT THEY CAN ALSO
CAUSE A STICKY SITUATION!
DON'T ADD TOO MUCH
MARGARINE AND BE SURE
TO COAT YOUR HANDS WITH
COOKING SPRAY BEFORE
YOU ROLL INTO BALLS. TO
TRANSPORT THESE WOBBLY
LITTLE WONDERS, I SUGGEST
CUTTING HOLES IN A SHOE
BOX SO THE CONES CAN
REST VERTICALLY WITHOUT
TIPPING OVER, OR BUYING A
BAKING RACK.

Simple Instructions

In a large microwave-safe bowl, melt margarine for 30 seconds to 1 minute.
Add marshmallows and microwave for 1½–2 minutes, stirring every 30 seconds. If you prefer, you can also melt marshmallows and margarine over
low heat in a large pan on the stove. Stir in cereal until completely coated
with the melted marshmallow. Let the mixture stand for 5 minutes so it is not
as sticky and unmanageable. Spray your hands with non-stick cooking
spray then form 12 balls with the mixture and place on wax paper. Let it
cool for about 30 minutes to set. Place each ball on top of a sugar cone
and serve. Secure with a little cake frosting if needed to help stick.

Hooray for the USA!

Make some magic for Memorial Day, create a festive Fourth of July, and show love for your country on Labor Day with these patriotic party treats.

USA SNACK MIX

MIX

Serves 4–6

This is a super easy snack mix to get you in the spirit. Mix and match ingredients to maximize the fun.

What You'll Need

You can use any combination of ingredients you like, but some of my favorites for the red, white, and blue effect include:

- POPCORN (PLAIN, NOT BUTTERED TO KEEP IT WHITE)
- MINI TWIST PRETZELS
- DRIED CRANBERRIES, CHERRIES, AND BLUEBERRIES
- WHITE CHOCOLATE CHIPS
- YOGURT-COVERED STAR COOKIES (CAN BE FOUND AT TRADER JOE'S)
- YOGURT COVERED PRETZELS
- RED & BLUE CANDY COATED CHOCOLATES (M&M'S OR OTHER)

Simple Instructions

Put your favorite ingredients in a large bowl. Stir and enjoy!

QUALITY TIME WITH THE KIDS: TURN YOUR SNACK MIX INTO A SWEETS & TREATS BUFFET. PLACE EACH OF THE INGREDIENTS IN ITS OWN SERVING BOWL AND PROVIDE SEASONAL CUPCAKE BAKING CUPS OR SMALL INDIVIDUAL CONTAINERS TO EACH CHILD. LET THEM HEAD DOWN THE LINE AND SELECT THEIR OWN SNACKS TO MAKE A CREATIVE CONCOCTION.

Fireworks
Popcorn

This super sweet treat is an explosion of happiness for your Fourth of July party or any summertime celebration.

What You'll Need

- 1 BAG MICROWAVE POPCORN, REGULAR FLAVOR
- 2 CUPS WHITE CHOCOLATE BAKING CHIPS, OR WHITE CANDY MELTS
- 1 PACKET STRAWBERRY POP ROCKS CANDY
- 1 PACKET BLUE RASPBERRY POP ROCKS CANDY

SUPER MOM SAYS: SINCE POP ROCKS CANDIES ARE A LITTLE "RETRO," THEY MAY BE A BIT HARD TO FIND. IF YOU ARE HAVING DIFFICULTY TRACKING DOWN BOTH COLORS, YOU CAN SUBSTITUTE ONE OF THEM WITH SUGAR SPRINKLES TO MAINTAIN THE RED, WHITE, AND BLUE COLOR SCHEME.

Simple Instructions

Pop microwave popcorn according to directions (being careful not to burn) and pour into large bowl to cool. Melt white chocolate chips or candy melts in a microwave-safe bowl 30 seconds at a time (up to 1½ minutes) on 50–60 percent power. Stir every 30 seconds. If white chocolate is too thick, add a little shortening and stir until smooth. Pour the melted white chocolate over the popcorn to taste and stir until coated. Sprinkle both colors of Pop Rocks on popcorn and mix. Cool to set and then serve.

SUMMER DIPPED STRAWBERRIES

Makes 12

Start with fresh strawberries from the season, add a dip of white chocolate and a splash of blue sprinkles to dress up these sweet berry treats for the Fourth of July!

What You'll Need
- 12 MEDIUM/LARGE FRESH STRAWBERRIES
- 2 CUPS WHITE CANDY MELTS, OR WHITE BAKING CHIPS
- BLUE SPRINKLES

Simple Instructions

Wash and completely dry the strawberries using a paper towel. Melt the white chocolate in a microwave-safe container on 50–60 percent power. Start with 1 minute. Stir. Continue in 30 second increments until melted and smooth. If necessary, add a tablespoon of shortening to help smooth. Dip strawberries ⅔ of the way in the melted chocolate and use a knife to help spread and smooth. Sprinkle each strawberry with blue sprinkles on the bottom third of the strawberry, leaving half of the white chocolate still showing to create a red, white, and blue effect. Lay on a plate coated with wax paper and place in the refrigerator to keep fresh.

LEARN FROM MY MISTAKES: THE FIRST TIME I MADE THESE, I HAD A LITTLE BIT OF TROUBLE APPLYING THE SPRINKLES. THE WHITE CHOCOLATE SHOULD BE SLIGHTLY HARDENED BEFORE YOU ATTEMPT TO DECORATE. I TRIED POURING THE SPRINKLES ONTO A PLATE AND ROLLING THE STRAWBERRIES TO COAT BUT IT ENDED UP REALLY CLUMPY. I FOUND THAT SPRINKLING AND TURNING THE STRAWBERRIES BY HAND WORKED BEST.

Sugar Cookie
SPARKLE CAKE

Serves 12–18

Shine like a star at your next patriotic party. This sugar cookie cake is super easy to make and takes no time at all to bake.

What You'll Need

- 2 TUBES REFRIGERATED SUGAR COOKIE DOUGH
- 1 CONTAINER WHITE CAKE FROSTING
- RED AND BLUE SUGAR SPRINKLES
- LARGE COOKIE PAN WITH RIMMED EDGES
- STAR-SHAPED COOKIE CUTTER(S)
- NON-STICK COOKING SPRAY

Simple Instructions

Spray the baking sheet with nonstick cooking spray. Spread both rolls of cookie dough onto the baking sheet and evenly distribute on the entire pan. Bake for 15–20 minutes at 350°F. Check on the cookie cake after about 15 minutes. To determine if it is done, stick a toothpick into the center and if it comes out clean, the cookie cake is fully baked. Cool completely then spread the white frosting to completely cover the top. Gently place the cookie cutter onto the frosting as a template and sprinkle inside with the colored sugar sprinkles. Remove the cookie cutter and the sprinkles will have formed a star shape. Repeat with red and blue sprinkles and various-sized cookie cutters until the top of the cookie cake is decorated to your liking.

QUALITY TIME WITH THE KIDS: KIDS LOVE SPRINKLES! GET YOUR KIDS INVOLVED WITH THE DECORATION OF THIS CUTE COOKIE CAKE AND LET THEIR INNER DESIGNERS COME OUT TO PLAY.

USA
PARFAIT

Makes 4-6 servings

Hooray for the USA! This kid-friendly dessert is a treat all summer long and can also be made with low-fat and low-sugar alternatives.

What You'll Need

- 1 PACKAGE RED JELL-O: RASPBERRY, STRAWBERRY, OR CHERRY
- 1 PACKAGE BLUE JELL-O: BERRY BLUE
- BOILING WATER
- COLD WATER
- ICE
- WHIPPED TOPPING (SUCH AS COOL WHIP)
- CLEAR PLASTIC CUPS

Prepare red and blue JELL-O in separate containers according to package directions. I prefer the quick set method with hot water, cold water, and ice). Cool in the refrigerator until it sets. Using a spoon, scoop the desired amount of red JELL-O into each plastic cup. With a different spoon, add a layer of whipped topping. Next create a layer of blue JELL-O, followed by a dollop of whipped cream. Enjoy.

QUALITY TIME WITH THE KIDS: LET THE KIDS MAKE THEIR OWN PATRIOTIC PARFAITS AS THEY ADD LAYERS OF EXCITEMENT. WATCH THEM JIGGLE AND GIGGLE AS THEY ENJOY.

STAR SPANGLED SODA

This recipe doubles as a refreshing drink and a great science experiment! A great addition to any cookout— Memorial Day, Fourth of July, or any summer celebration!

What You'll Need

- CRANBERRY JUICE OR FRUIT PUNCH (NOT DIET OR LIGHT, YOU NEED THE MOST SUGAR IN THIS SECTION!)
- BLUE SPORTS DRINK (SUCH AS GATORADE OR POWERADE)
- DIET 7UP
- ICE

Simple Instructions

Fill a cup completely with ice. Do not skip this step or the drink will not layer correctly. Slowly pour the drinks in equal amount into your glass. Start with the cranberry juice (the bottom layer should be the beverage with the most sugar). Next, gently pour the blue sports drink and then top with the clear Diet 7Up. Add a cherry for some added fun!

SUPER MOM SAYS: THE TRICK TO THIS MAGICAL DRINK IS RELATIVE DENSITY. THE BEVERAGE WITH THE MOST SUGAR STAYS ON THE BOTTOM AND THE LEAST SUGAR CONTENT FLOATS AT THE TOP. YOU CAN MAKE THIS COOL CONCOCTION THROUGHOUT THE YEAR USING DIFFERENT COLOR COMBOS AS LONG AS YOU LAYER YOUR DRINKS CORRECTLY.

MARSHMALLOW STAR BARS

Makes 8-12 stars

This recipe is a twist on traditional crispy marshmallow treats and is sure to be the star of your dessert table at your next patriotic party.

What You'll Need
- 6 CUPS CRISPY RICE CEREAL (LIKE RICE KRISPIES)
- 5½ CUPS MINI MARSHMALLOWS, OR 40 LARGE MARSHMALLOWS
- 3 TABLESPOONS MARGARINE OR BUTTER
- NON-STICK COOKING SPRAY
- RED AND BLUE SUGAR SPRINKLES, PATRIOTIC SPRINKLES, AND RED DECORATOR GEL
- MEDIUM-SIZED STAR-SHAPED COOKIE CUTTER

Simple Instructions
Microwave three tablespoons of butter or margarine in a large microwave-safe bowl on high for approximately 30 seconds or until melted. Add marshmallows, coat with melted butter, and then microwave for 1½–2 minutes, stirring every 30–45 seconds until marshmallows are melted. Add puffed rice cereal to the marshmallow mixture and stir until completely coated. Spray the bottom and sides of a 13 x 9-inch pan with non-stick cooking spray, then press the cereal mixture evenly into the pan. Let cool for 10–15 minutes and then use the star shaped cookie cutter to cut out star bars and place on wax paper. Decorate with rows of red and blue sprinkles, patriotic sprinkles, or decorator gel.

SUPER MOM SAYS: MARSHMALLOW CRISPY TREATS ARE ALWAYS A HIT AND CAN BE MADE WITHOUT ANY BAKING. JUST YOU, YOUR MICROWAVE, AND SOME OH-SO-FUN STAR SPANGLED SPRINKLES.

Berry Patriotic
CAKE

Serves 12-18

What's more patriotic and decadent than a cake that uniquely celebrates the United States of America? A star-spangled sweet to bring to a Memorial Day cookout, Fourth of July festivities, or your next summer block party!

What You'll Need
- 1 BOX YELLOW CAKE MIX
- INGREDIENTS TO PREPARE (I.E. EGGS, OIL, ETC.)
- 13 X 19-INCH BAKING PAN
- NON-STICK COOKING SPRAY
- 1 CONTAINER WHITE CAKE FROSTING
- 20-24 MEDIUM FRESH STRAWBERRIES
- 1 SMALL CONTAINER FRESH BLUEBERRIES

Simple Instructions

Preheat the oven and prepare the cake batter in a large mixing bowl according to cake mix instructions. Spray the bottom and sides of the baking pan with non-stick cooking spray. Pour the cake batter into the pan and bake following the package instructions.

While the cake is in the oven, wash and dry the strawberries and blueberries completely. Remove the stems of the strawberries and cut each vertically into even halves. Set aside. Once the cake has cooled the top and is no longer warm to the touch, cover the top with white cake frosting. Place blueberries in a square in the upper left corner of the cake to look like the stars on the American flag. Place strawberry halves from left to right in horizontal rows to make the red stripes of the flag.

LEARN FROM MY MISTAKES: WITH THE FRESH FRUIT ON THIS CAKE, IT IS IMPORTANT TO LET IT COMPLETELY DRY BEFORE USING IT TO DECORATE. IF THERE IS EXCESS WATER STILL ON THE BERRIES, THE COLOR WILL RUN AND YOUR FANTASTIC FLAG WILL TURN INTO A FLOP.

THE FRENZY OF FALL

As the warmth of summer fades and we transition into fall, the kids settle into their school routines and moms get to catch their breath . . . okay, maybe just for five minutes. One of the busiest times of year with after-school activities, homework, and work deadlines, there's hardly a moment to spare. Good news! You'll be fall-ing for these easy autumn recipes, which will help you keep your cool while you manage your busy calendar.

Easy-Breezy Autumn

Leave the ridiculous recipes behind when you create crafty and creative treats that celebrate the colors of fall.

Fall Harvest Party Mix

Fall Harvest Party Mix is a fun take on traditional party mixes. By adding candy corn and mini cornucopias, you instantly create a fabulous sweet and salty treat with a fall flair.

What You'll Need

Mix up your choice of the following ingredients. Improvise as you like!

- MINI PRETZEL TWISTS
- BUGLES BRAND SNACKS (CORNUCOPIAS)
- CANDY CORN
- COCKTAIL PEANUTS
- YOGURT RAISINS
- DRIED, SWEETENED CRANBERRIES
- MILK CHOCOLATE CHIPS AND BUTTERSCOTCH CHIPS
- POPCORN

Simple Instructions

Place your ingredients in a large bowl in desired quantities and give a good stir. Serve.

SUPER MOM SAYS: EVERY TIME I BRING THIS FESTIVE FALL SNACK MIX TO A PARTY, IT IS THE FIRST THING TO BE EATEN. JUST GOES TO SHOW YOU THAT THE AMOUNT OF TIME IT TAKES TO PREPARE DOES NOT DIRECTLY CORRELATE WITH POPULARITY!

Candy Corn
FRUIT CUPS

Makes 6

If you love candy corn but not all the sugar, this is a healthier alternative to bring to your child's class party that is still sweet to eat.

Simple Instructions

You will be creating three layers in each cup. Start by filling each cup a third full with pineapple chunks. Next add the mandarin oranges. Finally, add light whipped cream, top with once piece of candy corn and serve immediately.

What You'll Need

- 6 CLEAR PLASTIC CUPS
- 1 CAN PINEAPPLE CHUNKS (20 OZ)
- 1 CAN MANDARIN ORANGES (15–20 OZ)
- 1 CAN LIGHT WHIPPED TOPPING
- 6 CANDY CORNS (ONE FOR THE TOP OF EACH PARFAIT)

SUPER MOM SAYS: THIS RECIPE IS A FUN WAY TO GET THE KIDS TO EAT THEIR FRUIT AND THE RECIPE CAN ALSO SCALE VERY EASILY. DETERMINE HOW MANY KIDS YOU NEED TO SERVE AND THEN PURCHASE THE CORRECT NUMBER OF CANS OF FRUIT.

Too-Easy
Teepees

What You'll Need

- 8 SUGAR CONES
- 1 CONTAINER CHOCOLATE CAKE FROSTING (ROOM TEMPERATURE)
- FALL SPRINKLES
- 12 PRETZEL STICKS

QUALITY TIME WITH THE KIDS: THESE TEEPEES MAKE A TERRIFIC CENTERPIECE WHEN YOU COMBINE THEM WITH FALL LEAVES AND OTHER ACCESSORIES FOUND AROUND THE HOUSE. SEND YOUR KIDS ON A FALL SCAVENGER HUNT TO COLLECT YOUR DÉCOR.

Simple Instructions

Flip each sugar cone upside down, and with a knife carefully cut approximately ½ inch off the tip using a sawing motion. With a toothpick or small knife, place a dab of chocolate frosting on the inside rim of the cone where the tip was just removed. This will help secure the pretzels. Next, spread chocolate frosting around the outside of the larger part of the sugar cone, about ¼ to ½ inch thick. Apply fall sprinkles to decorate. Break each of the pretzel sticks into thirds. Insert three pieces into the small part of the cone so they are partially sticking out and secure to the frosting on the inside. Place the finished teepees in the refrigerator for a few minutes to set.

Mini Caramel
GRAPES

Makes 24

Everything seems more fun when you make them mini! These tiny treats are simple to make and are reminiscent of delicious caramel apples, which are so popular this time of year.

Simple Instructions

Remove the grapes from the vine and wash and dry completely. Insert a toothpick into the center of each grape. Unwrap the caramel candies and place in a microwave-safe bowl with two tablespoons of milk. Microwave the mixture for one minute. Remove from the microwave and let it sit for approximately one minute.

Holding the toothpick, carefully dip the entire grape into the caramel. If you would like to add toppings, crush the graham crackers into crumbs and place in a small bowl. Place chopped nuts in a separate bowl. Dip the bottom of the caramel grape into either one of the toppings and then place them on a plate covered with wax paper. Place in the refrigerator for about 20 minutes to set.

What You'll Need

- 24 MEDIUM TO LARGE GREEN GRAPES
- 24 TOOTHPICKS
- 1 BAG (14 OZ) INDIVIDUALLY WRAPPED CARAMELS
- 2 TABLESPOONS MILK
- 2–3 GRAHAM CRACKERS (OPTIONAL)
- CHOPPED NUTS (OPTIONAL)
- WAX PAPER

LEARN FROM MY MISTAKES: I FOUND THAT IT'S BEST TO WASH AND DRY YOUR GRAPES AN HOUR OR SO PRIOR TO DIPPING THEM INTO THE CARAMEL. IF THE GRAPES ARE STILL WET, THE OOEY, GOOEY CARAMEL WILL SLIDE RIGHT OFF. YOU CAN ALSO TYPICALLY FIND READY-MADE CARAMEL APPLE DIP AT THE GROCERY STORE THIS TIME OF YEAR, SO FEEL FREE TO USE IT IF YOU PREFER.

Perfect Pumpkin
APPLES

Makes 6

These tasty treats are perfect all season long. Keep them simple for a fall theme or add jack-o-lantern faces for Halloween parties.

What You'll Need

- 6 GRANNY SMITH APPLES
- 1 PACKAGE ORANGE CANDY MELTS (CAN BE PURCHASED AT A CRAFT STORE)
- 6 COOKIE POP STICKS OR POPSICLE STICKS
- ORANGE SUGAR SPRINKLES
- 6 MINI MARSHMALLOWS
- GREEN CUPCAKE DECORATOR ICING IN A CAN WITH STAR TIP
- WAX PAPER

Simple Instructions

Wash and completely dry each apple and firmly insert a cookie pop stick into the top center of each one. Set aside on wax paper. Melt orange candy melts in the microwave at 50 percent power for 2–3 minutes, stirring every 30 seconds, being careful not to overheat. Dip each apple into melted candies and turn to coat. Use a spoon to completely cover and smooth. Set on wax paper. After each apple is coated, sprinkle with orange sugar sprinkles. Push one mini marshmallow down the stick until it rests on top of the apple. Cover with green frosting to make the stem. Place in refrigerator for 15–20 minutes to set.

LEARN FROM MY MISTAKES:
THE FIRST TIME I TRIED TO MAKE THESE, I USED WHITE BAKING CHIPS AND THOUGHT I WOULD ADD FOOD COLORING DROPS TO MAKE THE MIXTURE ORANGE. BAD IDEA! WHEN I ADDED THE FOOD COLORING, A STRANGE REACTION OCCURRED AND THE WHOLE MIXTURE SEIZED UP AND WAS UNUSABLE. IT'S DEFINITELY BEST TO PURCHASE THE ORANGE CANDY MELTS, WHICH CAN BE FOUND AT CRAFT STORES.

PUMPKIN CUTIES

Makes 12

These mini pumpkins couldn't be any cuter, or easier to make. As a bonus, they are made from fresh fruit and veggies which make them good for the kids, too.

What You'll Need
- 12 MANDARIN ORANGES (CLEMENTINES)
- 1 STALK OF CELERY

Simple Instructions

Peel your clementines and set aside. Wash and completely dry your celery. Cut the celery stalk into small rectangles, about ½ inch long and ¼ inch wide. Stick the celery "stems" into the top of the clementines and serve.

QUALITY TIME WITH THE KIDS: HAVE THE KIDDOS HELP PEEL THE ORANGES WHILE YOU PREPARE THE CELERY "STEMS." YOU'LL BE DONE IN A FALL FLASH!

ADORABLE
Acorns

Makes 24

These bite-sized goodies will add at a festive look to your fall dessert table. They bring new meaning to fun finger food.

What You'll Need
- 24 MINI NILLA WAFERS
- 24 HERSHEY'S KISSES
- 24 BUTTERSCOTCH CHIPS
- 1 CONTAINER CHOCOLATE FROSTING

Simple Instructions

Unwrap all the Hershey's Kisses and set aside. One at a time, use a dinner knife to spread a small amount of the chocolate frosting onto the flat part of the Hershey's Kiss. Stick to the flat side of the Nilla Wafer. Using a tiny dab of chocolate frosting, secure the flat side of a butterscotch chip to the top of the Mini Nilla Wafer. Serve on a fall-colored platter.

SUPER MOM SAYS: THE FALLEN LEAVES ARE GORGEOUS THIS TIME OF YEAR SO USE THEM TO DRESS UP YOUR DESSERT DISPLAY. I LIKE TO LINE MY SERVING PLATE WITH A VARIETY OF LEAVES AND THEN PLACE THE ADORABLE ACORNS ON TOP FOR A COLOR POP.

Easy Owl
CUPCAKES

Makes 18-24

*Your kids will get a hoot out of these cute fall cupcakes.
They are outstanding for fall parties and celebrations.*

What You'll Need

- 1 BOX CHOCOLATE CAKE MIX
- INGREDIENTS TO PREPARE (I.E. EGGS, OIL, WATER, ETC.)
- 24 CUPCAKE BAKING CUPS
- 1 CONTAINER CHOCOLATE FROSTING
- 1 PACKAGE OREO COOKIES, OR OTHER CHOCOLATE SANDWICH COOKIES
- 1 LARGE BAG OF PLAIN M&M'S CHOCOLATE CANDIES, OR OTHER CANDY-COATED CHOCOLATES

Simple Instructions

Preheat the oven according to package instructions. Line the cupcake pan with the baking cups. Prepare the cupcake batter in a large bowl and pour into the baking cups, filling about ⅔ full. Bake the cupcakes as directed on the box. Cool completely and then top each with chocolate frosting.

Twist each OREO in half, trying to get as much frosting on one half as you can. You won't be using the unfrosted pieces. Place an M&M'S candy on the right center of one cookie and then the same colored candy on the left center of the second cookie. These will be the owl's eyes. Place the two OREO halves on top of each cupcake, frosting side out, with the M&M'S candies facing each other in the center. Place an orange M&M'S candy vertically in between and just below the eyes for the beak.

SUPER MOM SAYS:
ALTHOUGH THESE BIG-EYED OWLS TAKE A LITTLE LONGER THAN SOME OF THE OTHER RECIPES IN THIS BOOK, THEY MAKE AN OUTSTANDING IMPACT AND ARE WORTH THE EXTRA EFFORT.

Spooktacular
Halloween Sweets

These un-boolievably easy party treats have brought me much kudos at the kids' Halloween parties. There's nothing scary about these sweets that can be done in a snap!

Sweet & Salty
Spiders

These are creepy crawlies you won't be afraid to have in your home. Made with four simple store-bought ingredients, you'll be done in minutes instead of hours.

What You'll Need

- 1 PACKAGE BROWNIE BITES (USUALLY FOUND IN THE BAKERY SECTION OF THE GROCERY STORE)
- 1 PACKAGE LARGE PRETZEL TWISTS
- 1 PACKAGE CANDY EYES (FOUND IN BAKING SECTION)
- 1 CONTAINER CHOCOLATE FROSTING

Simple Instructions

Break the rounded edges off the pretzels into semi-circles that are about equal in length. Insert the tips of 6–8 pretzel pieces (3–4 on each side) into each brownie for the spider legs. Attach a pair of candy eyes to the top front of each brownie using a small dab of chocolate frosting.
Make as many as needed.

SUPER MOM SAYS: YES, I REALIZE THAT SPIDERS HAVE EIGHT LEGS. I HAVE FOUND THAT SIX LEGS TEND TO FIT BETTER INTO THESE BITE-SIZED BROWNIES. IF YOU ARE A STICKLER FOR ACCURACY, GO AHEAD AND TRY TO SQUEEZE THEM ALL IN!

Tombstone
Cupcakes

Makes 18–24

WITH THEIR EDIBLE TOMBSTONE AND CRUSHED COOKIE TOPPING, TOMBSTONE CUPCAKES ARE THE PERFECT HALLOWEEN TREAT THAT'S BOTH DECORATIVE AND DELICIOUS!

What You'll Need

- 1 BOX CHOCOLATE CAKE MIX
- INGREDIENTS TO PREPARE CAKE BATTER (I.E. EGGS, WATER, OIL)
- 1 CONTAINER CHOCOLATE FROSTING
- 1 PACKAGE OREO COOKIES, OR OTHER CHOCOLATE SANDWICH COOKIES
- 2 PACKAGES PEPPERIDGE FARM MILANO BRAND COOKIES, OR SIMILAR
- BLACK OR ORANGE DECORATOR ICING OR GEL
- GREEN SPRINKLES
- 18–24 CUPCAKE BAKING CUPS

SUPER MOM SAYS: THESE SPOOKTACULAR SWEETS HAVE BECOME A HALLOWEEN TRADITION IN OUR HOUSE. TRY TO COME UP WITH CREATIVE AND CLEVER SHORT SAYINGS TO ADORN YOUR TOMBSTONES . . . EEK!

Simple Instructions

Preheat the oven and prepare the cupcake batter according to package instructions.. Line the cupcake pan with the paper baking cups and fill each cup ⅔ full with batter. Bake cupcakes according to the time designated on the package. Remove from the oven and let cool completely.

Frost the top of each cupcake with chocolate frosting. Remove cream filling from the chocolate sandwich cookies using a knife and crush the cookies in a plastic bag to make "dirt." Sprinkle on top of each cupcake. Carefully cut each Milano cookie in half using a sawing motion to make tombstones. Write short expressions on each cookie with decorator gel (Boo, RIP, etc.). Gently insert the flat side of each cookie into the cupcake to make a tombstone on top of each. Decorate with green sprinkles to make "grass."

UnBOOlievable
LOW-FAT PUDDING TREATS

Makes 4

Surprise your kids with this creamy and chocolatey treat anytime during the Halloween season. So delicious they won't even realize this snack is actually low fat!

Simple Instructions

Remove foil covers from each pudding cup, being careful not to leave excess on the cups. Put whipped cream in a plastic bag and cut off about ½ inch from one corner. Carefully squeeze whipped cream on top of pudding in a circular motion to make the shape of a ghost. Add chocolate chips for the eyes and mouth with the flat part facing outward.

What You'll Need
- 4 FAT FREE (OR SUGAR FREE) PRE-PACKAGED CHOCOLATE PUDDING CUPS
- COOL WHIP LIGHT, OR COMPARABLE STORE BRAND
- 12 CHOCOLATE CHIPS OR MINI CHOCOLATE CHIPS
- 1 PLASTIC SANDWICH BAG

SUPER MOM SAYS: ADD THE WHIPPED CREAM TO THE TOPS OF THESE TREATS RIGHT BEFORE SERVING. THE WHIPPED CREAM GHOSTS TEND TO DEFLATE IF THEY SIT TOO LONG. NO ONE WANTS A GHASTLY LOOKING GHOUL!

FROZEN YOGURT BANANA GHOSTS

Makes 12

These spooky delicious treats will satisfy your children's sweet tooth and have them screaming for more. They are a super easy, healthy alternative for your little boys and ghouls!!

What You'll Need
- 6 MEDIUM-SIZED BANANAS (NOT OVERRIPE)
- 1 LARGE CONTAINER VANILLA GREEK YOGURT
- 24 BLACK CONFETTI SPRINKLES (THESE ROUND SPRINKLES USUALLY COME AS PART OF A MULTI-COLORED MIX), OR MINI CHOCOLATE CHIPS
- 12 COOKIE POP STICKS
- WAX PAPER

Simple Instructions
Cut each banana horizontally in half so there are two equal parts, pointed on one end and flat on the other. Insert a cookie pop stick into the flat bottom of each banana then place on a plate covered with wax paper. Freeze for 1–2 hours (you can freeze them overnight as well). Once frozen, dip the entire banana into the container of vanilla Greek yogurt and smooth out with a spoon until completely covered. Add two black circle sprinkle eyes to each and place back on the plate with wax paper. Put back in the freezer until the yogurt coating is frozen (at least one hour). Serve the same day and store extras in an airtight container to prevent freezer burn.

LEARN FROM MY MISTAKES: BE SURE TO FOLLOW THE STEPS LISTED ABOVE INCLUDING THE DOUBLE-FREEZING PROCESS. IF YOU ATTEMPT TO DIP UNFROZEN BANANAS IN THE YOGURT, YOUR GHOST MAY END UP LUMPY AND BUMPY. SCARY!

Friendly
Ghosts

What You'll Need

- 24 NUTTER BUTTER COOKIES
- 1 BAG WHITE CANDY MELTS OR WHITE CHOCOLATE BAKING CHIPS
- 1 TABLESPOON VEGETABLE SHORTENING (OPTIONAL)
- BLACK DECORATOR ICING OR BLACK CIRCLE CONFETTI SPRINKLES
- WAX PAPER

SUPER MOM SAYS: I STILL REMEMBER WHEN I BROUGHT THESE TO MY KIDS' HALLOWEEN PARTY A FEW YEARS BACK AND ONE OF THE MOMS SAID, "DID YOU MAKE THESE YOURSELF? THEY ARE ADORABLE!" WITH A SMILE, I SAID "YES, I MADE THEM!" SEE, EVEN SIMPLE SHORTCUTS CAN MAKE YOU LOOK LIKE A STAR.

Simple Instructions

In a microwave-safe container, melt the white candy melts or white chocolate chips at 50-60 percent power for approximately 1½ minutes, stirring every 45 seconds until melted. Do not overheat. If necessary, add one tablespoon of shortening to help smooth. Spoon the melted white chocolate over ¾ of each cookie on top and bottom and place on a plate covered with wax paper to cool. After the white chocolate has set for 2–3 minutes, place two black sprinkles for eyes or make eyes with black decorator frosting. Cool in the refrigerator.

Sweet & Salty
BROOMSTICKS

Makes 24

Your little witches and warlocks will love these sweet and salty treats at their next Halloween party and you'll like how quickly they can be created.

What You'll Need

- 24 REESE'S PEANUT BUTTER CUPS MINIATURES
- 24 PRETZEL STICKS
- DECORATOR GEL IN GREEN, ORANGE, OR PURPLE

Simple Instructions

Cool the Reese's Peanut Butter Cups miniatures in the refrigerator for 10–15 minutes to ensure that the chocolate is not too soft. After cooling, unwrap the peanut butter cups and be careful not to pull off the chocolate with the wrapper. Place them large side down on a plate. Insert pretzel sticks into the center of each peanut butter cup. Add a ring of color with decorator gel where the pretzel meets the chocolate. Store in the refrigerator.

QUALITY TIME WITH THE KIDS: USE THIS LITTLE RECIPE AS AN EXERCISE FOR YOUNGER KIDS IN COUNTING AND FINE MOTOR SKILLS. COUNT OUT THE CORRECT NUMBER OF CHOCOLATES, UNWRAP THEM CAREFULLY, AND THEN INSERT THE PRETZELS. WICKED FUN!

BOO
Brownies

Makes 12

Short on time? These little ghouls are an easy but festive semi-homemade treat to bring to your child's classroom party or family Halloween celebration.

What You'll Need
- 1 BOX BROWNIE MIX (OR YOU CAN BUY PRE-BAKED, UNFROSTED BROWNIES AT YOUR GROCERY STORE BAKERY)
- INGREDIENTS TO PREPARE BROWNIE MIX (I.E. EGG, OIL, WATER)
- 12 PEEPS GHOSTS
- 1 CAN GREEN CUPCAKE DECORATING ICING WITH STAR TIP
- 1 CONTAINER CHOCOLATE FROSTING

Simple Instructions

Preheat the oven. Prepare the brownie mix according to package directions and bake in a 9 x 9-inch or 9 x 13-inch pan. Let the brownies cool completely, cut into 12–18 squares, and carefully remove from the pan. Cut ¼ inch off the bottom of each Peeps ghost to make them flat. Attach the ghosts using chocolate frosting. In small pulses, apply the green decorating icing in a strip of green "grass" in front of the ghost where it connects to the brownie.

SUPER MOM SAYS: SKIP THE BAKING ALTOGETHER IF YOU ARE IN A RUSH. BUY PRE-MADE BROWNIES IN THE BAKERY SECTION OF YOUR LOCAL GROCERY STORE. IT'S NOT CHEATING . . . IT'S SUPER MOM SIMPLE!

Wickedly Easy
WITCH HATS

Makes 24

Need a quick treat to bring to your child's Halloween classroom party? This festive Halloween recipe can be completed in less than 15 minutes . . . I promise!

What You'll Need
- 24 CHOCOLATE-COVERED SHORTBREAD COOKIES
- 24 HERSHEY'S KISSES
- 1 CONTAINER CHOCOLATE FROSTING
- DECORATING GEL OR FROSTING IN HALLOWEEN COLORS (GREEN, ORANGE, PURPLE)
- HALLOWEEN SPRINKLES OR DECORATIONS
- WAX PAPER

Simple Instructions
Place the shortbread cookies face down on a tray covered with wax paper so the chocolate side is up. Unwrap the Hershey's Kisses and put a small amount of frosting on the flat side of the Kiss and place in the center of the cookie. Using decorating gel, pipe a circle around the bottom of the Hershey's Kiss where it connects to the cookie. Decorate as you like!

QUALITY TIME WITH THE KIDS: THESE ARE A FAN FAVORITE WITH MY KIDDOS. FORM A MINI-ASSEMBLY LINE AND EMPHASIZE TEAMWORK TO MAKE THESE CUTE CREATIONS. YOU'LL BE ABLE TO GET DOZENS DONE BEFORE YOU HAVE TO DASH OUT THE DOOR!

New Traditions for Your Thanksgiving Table

Whether you like pilgrims, pumpkins, or traditional apple pie, these bite-sized goodies will add a festive touch to your Thanksgiving dessert table.

Candy Corn Turkeys

Makes 12

These terrific Thanksgiving treats require no baking and are filled with personality. Before you know it, they will be gobbled right up!

What You'll Need

- 12 OREO COOKIES OR ROUND CHOCOLATE SANDWICH COOKIES
- 1 BAG CANDY CORN
- 24 CANDY EYES
- 12 CINNAMON DROP CANDIES
- 1 CONTAINER CHOCOLATE FROSTING

QUALITY TIME WITH THE KIDS: THESE TOO-CUTE TURKEYS CAN BE A FUN ACTIVITY FOR THE KIDS DURING THANKSGIVING BREAK. HAVE THEM HELP DECORATE AND COME UP WITH CREATIVE WAYS TO DISPLAY ON TURKEY DAY!

Simple Instructions

Holding the cookie vertically, carefully insert five candy corn pieces into the frosting on the top half to create the feathers. Next, use a dab of chocolate frosting and secure two of the edible candy eyes on the upper center of the cookie. Using another small amount of chocolate frosting on the larger end of the candy corn, place it vertically below the eyes to make the beak. Secure a single cinnamon drop candy off center underneath the beak with chocolate frosting to create the turkey's waddle. Display on a fall-themed or colored serving tray.

Pocket Apple
PIES

Makes 20-24

You can't have Thanksgiving without apple pie! Turn this traditional favorite into finger food that is perfect for holiday party munching.

Simple Instructions

Preheat the oven according to the directions on the pie crust package. Use the cookie cutter or jar lid to cut 5–6 circles of pie crust out of each sheet (20–24 circles total). Place the dough on cookie sheets and spoon a small amount of apple pie filling onto one half. Lightly sprinkle with cinnamon to taste. Fold each circle in half and pinch around the edges to seal. Sprinkle with colored sugar sprinkles to decorate. Bake for 12–15 minutes or until golden brown. Serve with whipped cream or vanilla ice cream.

What You'll Need
- 2 PACKAGES PRE-MADE REFRIGERATED PIE CRUSTS (2 SHEETS PER PACKAGE/4 SHEETS TOTAL)
- 2 CANS READY-MADE APPLE PIE FILLING
- SUGAR SPRINKLES IN FALL COLORS (GREEN, ORANGE, YELLOW)
- CINNAMON
- WHIPPED CREAM OR VANILLA ICE CREAM (OPTIONAL)
- LARGE ROUND COOKIE CUTTER OR JAR LID, APPROXIMATELY 3½–4 INCHES IN DIAMETER

SUPER MOM SAYS:
APPLE PIE IS ALWAYS A FAVORITE AT HOLIDAY MEALS, BUT SERVING IT CAN BECOME A STICKY SITUATION. THIS POCKET VERSION CREATES LESS MESS FOR BOTH YOUR GUESTS AND THE HOSTESS BECAUSE IT IS ALREADY IN PRE-PORTIONED SIZES.

Pilgrim Hat Treats

Makes 24

Complete your feast with these scrumptious choco-late-covered marshmallow cookies. Your little pilgrims will be thankful for these kid-friendly treats.

What You'll Need

- 24 LARGE MARSHMALLOWS
- 24 CHOCOLATE SHORTBREAD COOKIES
- 1 PACKAGE MILK CHOCOLATE CHIPS (12 OZ.)
- 1 TUBE OF WHITE, YELLOW, OR ORANGE DECORATOR ICING OR GEL
- 1 BAMBOO SKEWER
- WAX PAPER

Simple Instructions

Place the cookies chocolate side up on a wax paper–coated cookie sheet. Melt the chocolate chips in the microwave at 70–80 percent power for approximately 1½ minutes, stirring every 30 seconds until smooth. Place the marshmallow on a kabob stick or skewer and dip into the melted chocolate. Use a spoon to help coat the marshmallow completely. Gently place each marshmallow, flat side down, on top of each cookie. Cool in the refrigerator for at least 30 minutes to allow the chocolate to set. Remove from the refrigera-tor and use decorator frosting to draw a rectangular buckle on the front of each hat.

SUPER MOM SAYS:
STORE YOUR PILGRIM HAT TREATS IN A SEALED PLASTIC CONTAINER IN THE REFRIGERATOR TO KEEP THEM FRESH. REMOVE THEM FROM THE REFRIGERATOR AT LEAST ONE HOUR PRIOR TO SERVING TO GET THEM BACK TO ROOM TEMPERATURE.

Anytime
Celebrations

Looking for treats that can be used all season long? Look no further as the following recipes can be adapted to any occasion you find on your social calendar. With a simple color change and a cute container, these goodies are good to go!

Festive Fruit
Kabobs

THIS EASY AND HEALTHY PARTY RECIPE IS THE PERFECT TREAT TO SERVE WHEN YOU WANT TO SATISFY THE KIDS' SWEET TOOTH WHILE REDUCING THE AMOUNT OF SUGAR SERVED. USE FRUIT THAT IS IN SEASON AND COLOR COORDINATE FOR THE HOLIDAY.

What You'll Need
Choose a variety of fresh fruit from the current season like:

- SEEDLESS WATERMELON
- CANTALOUPE
- HONEYDEW MELON
- GREEN & PURPLE GRAPES
- STRAWBERRIES
- BLUEBERRIES
- PINEAPPLE
- BAMBOO SKEWERS
- SMALL SEASONAL COOKIE CUTTERS

SUPER MOM SAYS: THESE KABOBS LOOK BEST WHEN THEY ARE COLORFUL. FOR VALENTINE'S DAY, ALTERNATE WATERMELON HEARTS WITH STRAWBERRIES, BLUEBERRIES, AND RASPBERRIES. FOR SUMMER FUN, PICK TROPICAL FRUIT LIKE PINEAPPLE, GRAPES, AND STRAWBERRIES. HOSTING A PATRIOTIC PARTY? CREATE RED, WHITE, AND BLUEBERRY KABOBS WITH STRAWBERRIES, BLUEBERRIES, AND MINI MARSHMALLOWS.

Simple Instructions
Instead of just stacking seasonal fruit on a stick, try using a small seasonal cookie cutter to create fun shapes, and alternate with berries and grapes according to the holiday. To make fruit cut-outs, cut melon into slices ½ to ¾ inch thick and then press your small cookie cutter all the way through the melon. Gently push out the shaped pieces. (Watermelon is the easiest fruit to use for the cut-outs since there is no hole in the center of the melon.) Stack your fruit in the desired pattern on each bamboo skewer. Store the fruit kabobs in an air-tight container in the refrigerator until ready to serve. Delicious and nutritious!

Easy Ice
CREAM PIE

Serves 8

This simply super sweet treat will be a hit with your guests during any season. Better yet, it takes only minutes to prepare, although your friends and family will think you've spent hours in the kitchen.

Simple Instructions

Allow the ice cream to sit out on the counter for about 20–30 minutes so it will soften. Empty the softened ice cream into a large mixing bowl and gently stir until it reaches a smooth consistency. Gently spread the ice cream into the cookie pie crust so it is evenly distributed, being careful not to damage the crust. Add sprinkles or other seasonal decorations to your liking. Place the ice cream pie into the freezer to set for at least one hour. Remove and add a ring of whipped topping around the entire edge.

What You'll Need

- 1 PRE-MADE OREO COOKIE PIE CRUST
- 1 CARTON OF ICE CREAM (SELECT YOUR FLAVOR BASED ON THE HOLIDAY)
- 1 CAN OF WHIPPED TOPPING
- SPRINKLES, CHOCOLATE SYRUP, OR SEASONAL DECORATIONS

SUPER MOM SAYS: THERE ARE UNLIMITED VARIATIONS OF THIS PIE SO BE SURE TO USE YOUR IMAGINATION. FOR CHRISTMAS, TRY PEPPERMINT ICE CREAM. FOR ST. PATRICK'S DAY TRY MINT CHOCOLATE CHIP, AND FOR HALLOWEEN AND THANKSGIVING, PUMPKIN ICE CREAM PIE . . . YUM!

Candied Kiss
PRETZELS

1-2-3! These super simple, three-ingredient chocolate pretzel treats can be made in minutes. They are an easy and time-saving option when you need to bring a dessert in a pinch to a party.

What You'll Need
- 24 SQUARE OR ROUND PRETZELS
- 24 HERSHEY'S KISSES
- M&M'S CHOCOLATE CANDIES OR CANDY-COATED CHOCOLATES (HOLIDAY COLORS)

Simple Instructions

Preheat the oven to 175°F. Lay the pretzels in a single layer on a cookie sheet. Unwrap all the Hershey's Kisses. Place one chocolate on top of each pretzel. Put the cookie tray in the oven for approximately 5–10 minutes. The Hershey's Kisses should be soft but not completely melted (still holding their shape). Remove from the oven and gently press one M&M into the top of each Hershey's Kiss to flatten a bit. Let cool for 5–10 minutes and then place in a single layer on a plate or in a plastic container and refrigerate for 10 minutes to set the chocolate. Remove from the refrigerator and store in a plastic container at room temperature until ready to serve.

QUALITY TIME WITH THE KIDS: "MOM, I'M BORED!" THE THREE WORDS MOTHERS DREAD. PUT YOUR LITTLE ANGELS TO WORK BY HAVING THEM UNWRAP THE HERSHEY'S KISSES AND PLACE THEM ON THE PRETZELS BEFORE THEY GO IN THE OVEN.

COLORFUL CHOCOLATE PRETZELS

Makes 24

This easy recipe is one of the go-to items in my sweet treats arsenal. Instead of bringing a plate of cookies, surprise your hostess with these deliciously decadent and pretty pretzels.

What You'll Need
- 24 PRETZEL RODS
- 1 PACKAGE CHOCOLATE CHIPS (MILK CHOCOLATE OR SEMI-SWEET)
- A VARIETY OF DECORATIONS FOR THE SEASON – SPRINKLES, DECORATOR GELS, M&M'S, OR OTHER CANDY-COATED CHOCOLATES, ETC.
- WAX PAPER

Simple Instructions

Cover a baking sheet with wax paper. Melt the chocolate chips in the microwave on 70–80 percent power for approximately 1½ minutes until smooth. Stir every 30–45 seconds. Dip the pretzel rods into the melted chocolate and coat ⅔ of the pretzel using a spoon. Smooth off excess. Lay the pretzel flat on the wax paper and let the chocolate set for approximately 1–2 minutes before applying sprinkles or decorations. Decorate as you like with candies, sprinkles, and decorator gel. Let cool completely before removing from wax paper.

QUALITY TIME WITH THE KIDS: THIS RECIPE IS ONE OF MY KIDS' FAVORITES TO MAKE AND EAT. LEAVE THE CHOCOLATE DIPPING TO MOM AND THEN HAVE THE KIDS USE THEIR CREATIVITY TO DECORATE. FOR SEASONAL FUN, TRY ADDING CRUSHED CANDY CANES FOR CHRISTMAS, CONVERSATION HEART CANDIES FOR VALENTINE'S DAY, AND USA-COLORED SPRINKLES FOR THE FOURTH OF JULY.

Makes 12

These yummy sweets-on-a-stick add a multitude of colors to any party or occasion. Arrange them in a festive vase and they can also serve as a fun centerpiece for your party.

What You'll Need

- 12 BAMBOO SKEWERS
- 12 LARGE MARSHMALLOWS
- ASSORTED COLORS OF SUGAR SPRINKLES AND SEASONAL SPRINKLES
- 1 BAG MILK CHOCOLATE CHIPS
- DECORATOR GEL
- WATER

LEARN FROM MY MISTAKES: IF YOU ARE MAKING POPS IN A VARIETY OF COLORS, IT'S BEST TO DRY THEM CLUSTERED IN INDIVIDUAL COLORS (I.E. YELLOWS TOGETHER IN ONE TALL GLASS, GREENS IN ANOTHER GLASS). THE COLORED SUGAR SPRINKLES HAVE A TENDENCY TO TRANSFER FROM ONE MARSHMALLOW TO ANOTHER IF THEY ARE STILL WET.

Simple Instructions

There are two versions of these festive marshmallow pops that you can try: Sparkle Pops and Choco Pops. Start by placing a marshmallow on the top of each bamboo skewer. For the Sparkle Pops, fill a cup with water and dip the entire marshmallow into the water for 5 seconds. Over the top of a plate, immediately sprinkle each marshmallow with a generous amount of colored sugar sprinkles. Let them dry vertically by placing in a tall cup.

For the Choco Pops, melt the chocolate chips in the microwave on 70–80 percent power for approximately 1½ minutes until smooth. Stir every 30–45 seconds. Dip the marshmallows on the skewers into the melted chocolate. Use a spoon to cover the entire marshmallow with the chocolate. Place the skewer in a tall glass (marshmallow sticking out of the top) to set the chocolate for 1–2 minutes. If you are adding sprinkles, apply them before putting the marshmallow pops in the refrigerator to cool. If applying decorator gel, allow pops to chill in the refrigerator for 30 minutes to set the chocolate and then apply gel.

CELEBRATION COOKIE
Pops

Makes 12–18

Brighten a friend or family member's day with these pretty cookie pops. Get the kids involved with the decorating and spend some quality time together.

Simple Instructions

Preheat the oven and prepare the cookie dough as indicated on the package for cutout cookies. Use extra flour as necessary so the dough is not too sticky. Flour a clean, dry surface and roll out the cookie dough to approximately ¼ inch thick. Press the cookie cutter into the dough and trim the edges. Place approximately 8 cookie pop sticks on each baking sheet leaving ample space in between. Transfer the cut out cookie dough using a spatula and gently place each cookie on top of a stick with at least 1½–2 inches of cookie overlapping the stick. Press down gently on the cookie dough to ensure the stick attaches. Leave at least 1 inch in between each cookie on the pan as they will expand when baking.

If you are planning to decorate with sprinkles (no frosting), add the sprinkles before baking. If you prefer to frost the cookies, bake according to package directions. Let cool on the baking sheet for two minutes then gently use a spatula to remove from the pan and place on aluminum foil. Decorate with frosting and sprinkles once completely cooled. Store the cookies in an air tight container to keep fresh.

What You'll Need
- MEDIUM TO LARGE SEASONAL COOKIE CUTTERS (HEARTS, FLOWERS, SNOWFLAKES, PUMPKINS)
- 1 BAG PACKAGED SUGAR COOKIE MIX
- INGREDIENTS TO PREPARE COOKIE MIX (I.E. 1 STICK BUTTER, 1 EGG)
- FLOUR
- 18 COOKIE POP STICKS OR POPSICLE STICKS
- CAKE FROSTING (VARIOUS COLORS FOR THE SEASON)
- SEASONAL SPRINKLES
- BAKING SHEET

QUALITY TIME WITH THE KIDS: THIS IS A GREAT ACTIVITY TO INCLUDE THE KIDS IF YOU HAVE A LITTLE PATIENCE AND DON'T MIND A BIT OF A MESS! LET THEM FROST AND DECORATE THE COOKIES WITH THEIR OWN PERSONAL DESIGNS AND THEN DISPLAY IN A GLASS OR VASE ON THE KITCHEN TABLE FOR ALL TO ENJOY.

INDEX